Everyone Needs a Mentor

Fostering talent in your organisation

4th edition

Professor David Clutterbuck is one of Europe's most prolific and well-known management writers and thinkers. He has written more than 40 books and hundreds of articles on cutting edge management themes. Co-founder of The European Mentoring and Coaching Council and of The Item Group (a leading provider of internal communication solutions), he also runs a thriving international consultancy, Clutterbuck Associates, which specialises in helping people in organisations develop the skills to help others. He is perhaps best-known in recent years for his work on mentoring, on which he consults around the world. His books on mentoring include the classic *Everyone needs a mentor*, *Learning Alliances*, *Mentoring in Action*, and *Mentoring executives and directors*. The broad scope of his work can be seen on the Clutterbuck Associates and item websites www.clutterbuckassociates.co.uk and www.item-.co.uk. David can also be contacted by e-mail on dclutterbuck@item.co.uk.

The Chartered Institute of Personnel and Development is the leading publisher of books and reports for personnel and training professionals, students, and all those concerned with the effective management and development of people at work. For details of all our titles, please contact the publishing department:

tel: 020–8612 6200

fax: 020–8612 6201

e-mail: publish@cipd.co.uk

The catalogue of all CIPD titles can be viewed on the CIPD website:

www.cipd.co.uk/bookstore

Everyone Needs a Mentor

Fostering talent in your organisation

4th edition

David Clutterbuck

Chartered Institute of Personnel and Development

Published by the Chartered Institute of Personnel and Development, 151 The Broadway,
London, SW19 1JQ

First published 1985

Second edition 1991

Third edition 2001

This edition published 2004

Reprinted 2006(twice), 2008(twice), 2009, 2010, 2011, 2012

Design by Beacon GDT, Mitcheldean, Gloucestershire
Typeset by Kerrypress, Luton, Bedfordshire
Printed in Great Britain by Short Run Press Ltd, Exeter

British Library Cataloguing in Publication Data
A catalogue of this publication is available from the British Library

ISBN 978-18439-80544

The views expressed in this publication are the author's own and may not necessarily reflect those of the CIPD.

The CIPD has made every effort to trace and acknowledge copyright holders. If any source has been overlooked, CIPD Enterprises would be pleased to redress this for future editions.

Chartered Institute of Personnel and Development,
151 The Broadway,
London, SW19 1JQ
Tel: 020 8612 6200   Fax: 020 8612 6201

Contents

Figures and Tables

Preface

This is the 4th edition of *Everyone Needs a Mentor*, and I am still amazed by how much more there is to say on the topic. In the past two years there has been a significant increase in the quantity and quality of mentoring at a distance, particularly by e-mail. Academic research, particularly in Europe, has given us valuable clues on key aspects of mentoring relationship management. There have been major moves to establish good practice standards across the world. And, again in Europe, the leading proponents of coaching and mentoring have recognised the value of combining resources and learning, forming the European Mentoring and Coaching Council. Already this body is having an influence over practice in both disciplines in Australasia and South Africa.

In this revision, we begin with a detailed review of the evolution of structured mentoring programmes, from their origins in the United States to their continued evolution in Europe and the rest of the world. We explore definitions of mentoring and the key differences between the two prevailing philosophies of mentoring – sponsoring and developmental.

Chapter 2 looks at the dynamics that underlie the two main models of mentoring and places them into the wider context of developmental alliances.

Chapter 3 opens up the vexed issue of formality versus informality. Just how much structure and management does a formal scheme need to approach the performance of a really effective informal relationship?

Chapter 4 explores the benefits of mentoring, from the point of view of four key stakeholders – the employer, the mentee, the mentor and the mentee's colleagues.

Chapter 5 examines the competencies of both mentor and mentee – what they do and the skills they need to extract the maximum value from this powerful developmental environment.

Chapter 6 covers the issues of selection and matching, providing some ground rules for managing both processes.

Chapter 7 deals with the basics of designing and initiating a programme, from setting clear goals, through training for all participants, to communication and securing adequate championship.

Chapter 8 focuses on how to ensure that the programme is self-sustaining. Although many programmes are designed to have a finite life, because they tackle specific business or social issues, it is important that they remain dynamic and vital for that period.

Chapter 9 is a new chapter, bringing together the rapid developments in standards for mentoring programmes and introducing the new International Standards for Mentoring Programmes in Employment.

Chapter 10, also a new chapter, investigates another new phenomenon: the expansion of peer and upward (reverse) mentoring programmes.

Chapter 11 details how the typical successful mentoring relationship develops over time, and explores some of the implications this has for programme management.

Chapter 12 continues the management theme by illustrating some of the most common problems that occur within the mentoring relationship and within the mentoring scheme, and suggests ways of avoiding those problems.

Mentoring graduate recruits, explored in **Chapter 13**, is one of the longest-established applications of mentoring and is a priority area for many organisations. Mentoring has reduced turnover of graduate recruits by two-thirds and more in their first 12 months.

Chapter 14, which looks at the specific and rapidly growing area of mentoring in support of diversity, includes a new case study of one of the most innovative schemes, by the Audit Commission.

Chapter 15 addresses another rapidly growing area of application: mentoring at the most senior levels of organisations. Human resource directors are increasingly challenging the efficacy of individual relationships – and this, in turn, is driving the demand for professionalisation and measurement of the executive mentor role.

Chapter 16 examines the practicalities and potential for e-mentoring. Initial scepticism about the effectiveness of e-mentoring is fading as experience shows it has advantages as well as disadvantages.

The advice given in *Everyone Needs a Mentor* is based on nearly 30 years of research and practical experience in helping organisations in many parts of the world to design and implement mentoring programmes.

I have been lucky enough to work and exchange learning over this time with a remarkable array of academics and practitioners. Among the academics (at the risk of offending those I miss out) are Kathy Kram, whose original research in Boston was so influential in popularising structured mentoring programmes, Belle Rose Ragins, Liz Borredon, David Megginson, Bob Garvey, Stephen Gibb, Terri Scandura, Monica Higgins, Anthony Grant, Truls Engström, Unn Solle and Jennybeth Ekeland. Among the practitioners, Jenny Sweeney, Kim Langridge, Linda MacGregor and the entire team of colleagues at Clutterbuck Associates. I have also been lucky enough to learn from a host of clients, whose enthusiasm for mentoring has fuelled my own.

I hope this new edition of *Everyone Needs a Mentor* will prove as useful in supporting mentoring programmes as the previous three. It has not escaped my notice that the time between revisions seems to halve on each occasion. I guess I should be thinking about the 5th edition now!

David Clutterbuck

Part 1:

Introduction

1

The what and why of mentoring

I have been lucky enough to have had a number of mentors over the years, although it is only in recent decades that I have fully recognised and appreciated the role that some of these people played. I have also been fortunate to have been mentor to a wide range of people from different backgrounds and age groups. I am grateful for the learning I have received from them and for the feeling of privilege in helping them achieve goals very different from my own.

'Gratitude', 'learning' and 'privilege' are three terms we hear frequently, when people talk about their experiences as mentor or mentee. The need to learn and the need to help others to learn are deep-seated emotional drives within most people. These drives were a part of human evolution. It seems that a distinguishing feature between *homo sapiens sapiens* (us) and other species of great ape is the instinct on the one hand to pass on abstract learning or wisdom, and on the other to receive it. Our liking for story and anecdote – which are closely associated with depth and quality of learning – is no accident. As accumulated wisdom was passed from one generation to another, it expanded the range of human ability and opened up an ever-increasing gulf between humanity and the rest of the animal kingdom.

That instinct is a double-edged sword, however. It often occurs that the desire of the more experienced person (especially if he or she is much older) to pass on accumulated wisdom exceeds greatly the desire of the less experienced person to listen. Most people may have the instinct to be a mentor, but to do the role well requires a capacity to hold back and allow people to learn for themselves.

From reading much of the early literature on mentoring it would be easy to conclude that the mentor is someone who gives wise advice – indeed, that is one of the common dictionary definitions. In practice, mentors provide a spectrum of learning and supporting behaviours, from challenging and being a critical friend to being a role model, from helping to build networks and develop personal resourcefulness to simply being there to listen, from helping people work out what they want to achieve, and why, to planning how they will bring change about. A mentor may also be a conscience, a friend and – in certain definitions – a godfather or sponsor.

It is the holistic nature of the mentoring role that distinguishes it from other learning or supporting roles, such as coaching or counselling. We explore the differences in detail in

Chapter 2, but suffice for now to say that although mentoring shares behaviours with some styles of coaching and some styles of counselling, the overlap of roles is only partial. A number of sports now provide top athletes with a mentor as well as a coach. Whereas the coach concentrates on technique and motivation, the mentor provides a very different kind of support – one based on reflective learning and something akin to pastoral care.

A key capability of the effective mentor is being able to adapt to a much wider range of behaviours.

There is also a remarkable width to the range of applications for mentoring. Examples of mentoring programmes in recent years include:

- The International Labour Organisation uses mentoring to help its young professionals (typically highly qualified people in their mid- to late twenties) become acclimatised to the organisation in their first year. After their induction year, they are normally assigned to the field. They find it can be very important to have a trusted confidant(e) back at headquarters.

- The Public Sector Leaders Scheme is a development programme run by the Cabinet Office to support senior Civil Servants in growing their leadership skills. Every participant in the course has the opportunity to be mentored. Participants can choose to have a mentor for the duration of the scheme and beyond. The Secretariat has a pool of mentors from senior levels in the public sector. PSLS participants can select their own mentor from a choice of three (from a pool selected by the Secretariat), introduce a current mentor to PSLS, or continue to work with their current mentor if they have one.

- Ericsson, the Swedish mobile telephone company, uses a global mentoring programme aimed at international high-flyers, helping them to become comfortable in a global culture.

- BOOST is an innovative project in Zimbabwe to help the brightest, most entrepreneurial graduates set up their own businesses, which in turn hire other graduates. Against a background of political turmoil and very high unemployment among graduates, the scheme has received considerable backing at home and abroad. The mentors are all successful businesspeople from the local economy.

- British Aerospace, which recruits some 400 graduates annually, aims to give each of them a mentor for at least the first year.

- The Cabinet Office manages a programme for unleashing the potential of people with severe disability. It pairs the disabled person with a more senior Civil Servant, who can help him or her think constructively about issues of career management and personal development.

- A major London solicitor's practice uses mentoring to help people make the transition to partner. What it takes to be considered partner material is so difficult to explain or demonstrate that formal training does not really help.

Mentoring provides a useful way of passing on this largely intuitive understanding.

- For Shell in Brunei and elsewhere, a major challenge is how to speed up the development of local nationals to take over from the expatriate engineers and managers. Mentoring provides a practical and culturally acceptable route towards making this happen.

- The World Bank attracts the best and brightest people from around the world, making it a hothouse of ideas and potential cultural conflict. From a handful of relationships two years ago, mentoring has spread to some 2,000 pairs, in a variety of schemes, each either providing a support network for a particular ethnic or functional group, or building bridges between them.

- Birmingham's BEAT scheme, which addressed the special needs of young people leaving prison, placed most of its youngsters into work and kept them out of court. In addition, some of the mentors were long-term unemployed people who gained so much self-confidence helping the young offenders into employment that they, too, returned to full-time work.

- FAS, the Irish Ministry of Employment, is helping thousands of difficult-to-employ young people – many of them from families with no history of stable employment for generations – to acquire self-confidence and skills with a combination of FAS-delivered training, coaching from colleagues in their work placement and mentoring from a senior manager in the placement company.

- Mentors help musically talented young people stick to it through the difficult teenage years when other attractions tug at their attention.

- There are now a number of programmes where volunteers from local companies or from the community in general spend time helping children with poor literacy and numeracy skills to catch up. (There is some debate about whether this is really mentoring, even where there is an additional role of helping the young person think about life goals, but we'll avoid that for now.)

- Black students at risk of dropping out of university may have a mentor for the first year to help them settle in.

- Some schools now provide each newcomer with a peer mentor from two years above to help him or her settle in. The arrangement also helps build the self-respect and maturity of the young mentor. Another group increasingly targeted within schools as potential mentees is children at risk from bullying.

Crime Concern has used mentoring to target young people at risk. Similar programmes in the United States show that having an adult to share concerns with and be a positive role model has a major positive effect upon absenteeism, violent behaviour, drug abuse and the young person's relationships in general. Other schemes offering similar support include 100 Black Men, where the mentors are drawn from the same ethnic group as the young people at risk.

Mentoring schemes targeted at legitimate refugees (who have been given permission to remain in the UK) have helped these people and their families settle in to their new lives more rapidly and with greater confidence.

The notion that *everyone needs a mentor* is not so far from the truth. At key times in our lives, having a mentor can make a substantial difference to the choices we make, how confident we feel in making them, and how likely we are to achieve what we want.

THE BUSINESS CASE IN BRIEF

We explore the benefits to employers, mentees, mentors and third parties more fully in Chapter 4 and in Appendix 1, so this is simply a brief summary. Employer organisations have found that having a well-run mentoring scheme has a significant, positive impact upon both recruitment and retention. In some cases, the loss of young graduates in their first year has been cut by two-thirds, simply because there is someone outside the authority structure who has the interest to listen and the breadth of perspective to help the mentee make wise and confident choices.

Other employer benefits relate to having more effective succession planning, helping employees cope with the stresses of major change, and increasing productivity.

Mentees report a wide range of benefits, ranging from speed of settling in to a new role to deeper understanding of their own motivations. Recent research has led us to categorise the benefits to mentees in four ways:

- development outcomes, which may include knowledge, technical competence and behavioural competence

- career outcomes, which may include the achievement (in part or whole) of career goals

- enabling outcomes, such as having a career plan, a (self)-development plan, a wider network of influencers or learning resources

- emotional outcomes – less tangible, but often powerful changes in emotional state, including increased confidence, altruistic satisfaction, reflective space, status and the pleasure of a different kind of intellectual challenge.

These same benefits seem to apply broadly to mentors as well. The principal benefit described by mentors in successful developmental mentoring relationships is the learning they acquire from the experience. (This is not the case in sponsorship mentoring (see Chapter 2). A recent survey by Sandia Laboratories in the United States did not list 'own learning' as a benefit at all. This is not unexpected in a style of mentoring where the authority and power of the mentor are seen as important elements in the emotional contract.) Second comes the satisfaction from helping someone else – the vicarious pleasure of seeing someone else succeed.

Third parties, such as line managers and work colleagues, benefit because the mentee has someone with whom to discuss how he or she builds and maintains better working relationships. One recent case reported to me by a colleague concerns a man who explained that his reason for seeking a mentor was to help him get out from under his boss, for whom he had very little respect. After six months, the mentoring pair agreed to change the objective. By reflecting on the relationship with his boss and working to improve it, he had eventually realised that this person had much to teach him and that they could get along together pretty well.

Outside the work environment, mentoring has had a remarkable influence on the lives of a wide spectrum of disadvantaged or dispossessed people.

When I originally wrote this book, I debated whether *Everyone Needs a Mentor* was truly accurate as a title. After all, perhaps there were people who could live their lives without any recourse to such external help. I have yet to find anyone who is self-sufficient enough not to benefit from having a mentor at some point in his or her life. What I have found is many thousands of people who wish they could have had a mentor at formative periods or times of critical personal transition. It is gratifying that most of these people are willing to give others what they did not have. Perhaps another definition of mentoring might be 'Man's humanity to Man' (in the generic sense of 'Man', of course!).

Part 2:

Establishing a mentoring programme

2

Models and methods of mentoring

One of the biggest problems in trying to understand the mentoring phenomenon is pinning down exactly what is meant by the term. The confusion has arisen for several reasons. Firstly, the development of mentoring concepts and behaviours has been strongly influenced by culture – both organisational and national.

Secondly, other forms of one-to-one developmental help, such as coaching, have also had a rapid evolution in recent years. The range of styles open to coaches has expanded from a traditional 'Go try this, and I'll give you feedback on how you performed' approach or a 'Watch me, then you try it' approach to styles that place much more emphasis on questioning, stimulative techniques. It is not that coaching has invaded mentoring's territory, or vice versa. While the roles have remained separate, the behavioural repertoire available to each has increased over the past two decades.

A third reason for the confusion is that many of the academics who have studied mentoring have been – let's not mince words – pretty sloppy in their approach to defining what they are talking about. There seems to have been a general assumption that everyone knows what mentoring is, so there's no need to bother defining it. The reality is very different. The purpose of the relationship, the expectations of the mentoring pair, and the context in which they operate, all contribute to substantial differences in style and definition.

In some cases, mentoring is seen as an activity that can take place within the line of command; in others, this is seen as incompatible with the fundamental openness of the relationship. In some cultures, the exercise of authority and influence on the part of a protégé is seen as appropriate; in others, it is seen as primarily a developmental activity, with the emphasis on empowering and enabling people to do things for themselves. Some people view mentoring as synonymous with coaching; others see it as a form of counselling. Yet others view it as a kind of godfather relationship.

Dr Audrey Collin (1979), of the School of Management at Leicester Polytechnic, gathered a number of largely US definitions of mentoring for an article in *Personnel Review* magazine. Mentors were said, for example, to be 'influential people who significantly help you reach your major life goals'. Mentoring is 'a process in which one person [the mentor] is responsible for overseeing the career and development of another person [the mentee] outside the normal manager/subordinate relationship'. Alternatively, mentoring was 'a protected relationship in which learning and experimentation can occur, potential skills can be developed, and in which results can be measured in terms of competencies gained rather than curricular territory covered'.

Subsequent definitions have included:

The basic model of mentoring is that one person passes their greater knowledge and wisdom to another.

(Hay, 1995)

A mentor is a professional person who is a wise, experienced, knowledgeable individual who 'either demands or gently coaxes' the most out of the mentee.

(Caruso, 1992)

... a one-to-one relationship in which a senior manager oversees the development and progression of a more junior manager

(Equal Opportunities Review, 1995)

... an experienced, objective sounding-board with the power to influence events

(Conway, 1995)

... to help and support people to manage their own learning in order to maximise their potential, develop their skills, improve their performance, and become the person they want to be

(Parsloe, 1992)

And finally, a definition from our own work:

... off-line help from one person to another in making significant transitions in knowledge, work or thinking

(Megginson and Clutterbuck, 1995)

All of these definitions are valid in the specific context which they were intended to describe. None, however, can truly be said to be generic – equally applicable in all situations. As with most definitions of complex phenomena, the more generic they are, the vaguer they tend to be!

A fundamental warning for anyone attempting to make sense of mentoring by reading the academic journals is that if a piece does not explicitly identify the type of relationship and the objectives of the relationship, it is likely to be at best misguided and probably misleading.

Terms like 'oversee' and 'responsible for' project an image of a hands-on kind of relationship with a clear sense of senior and subordinate. The word 'protégé' also carries distinct overtones of applied power. These concepts are carried on into most of the North American and some European academic literature on mentoring, and in particular, in how mentoring success is measured. It is worth at this point making the controversial but in my view accurate point that *the vast majority of US literature on mentoring is of minimal value in planning and understanding mentoring in a European context* because it begins from fundamentally different assumptions about the role and nature of mentoring. Mentoring schemes in the UK and Europe, and to a large extent in Australia/New Zealand, tend to conform to a model that emphasises mutuality of learning and the encouragement of the mentee to do things himself or herself; and to a much broader vision of both the role of the mentor and the interactivity between mentor and mentee.

The definition referred to above from our own work – 'off-line help from one person to another in making significant transitions in knowledge, work or thinking' – has become the most commonly accepted for this developmentally oriented and empowering approach to mentoring. The rationale behind the component words and phrases is as follows:

- 'Off-line' is appropriate because it is difficult to be fully open in a relationship where one person has authority over the other. In the few cases where mentoring relationships have been set up between individuals and their managers, the managers in particular have found a conflict of role: either the mentees hold back information or the managers find themselves in possession of confidences which they cannot use without damaging the relationship. There are rare occasions when an off-line mentoring relationship becomes an in-line relationship and, if it is sufficiently strong, may continue informally. However, most schemes would withdraw support for a formal mentoring relationship in these circumstances.

- 'Help' is a weak term, but it covers a wide range of resources for which the mentee can turn to the mentor – from direct advice to simply listening. A key skill for the effective mentor is to be able to adapt the nature of the help given to the mentee's needs at the time.

- 'One person to another': in developmental mentoring the hierarchy is not important – it is the experience gap that matters. Peer mentoring is increasingly common, as is upward mentoring, where the mentor is more junior in terms of the hierarchy. Top management at GE all have young e-literate mentors who keep them abreast of new technology. Two short cases at the end of this chapter illustrate upward mentoring in more detail.

- 'Significant transitions': mentoring schemes and mentoring relationships need some sense of purpose if they are to achieve benefits for the participants. We explore some of this in Chapters 7 and 8. One of the most common problems with formal mentoring schemes is that mentor and mentee meet, each hoping the other will define what they should be talking about. This is not a recipe for success!

A relatively concise description of the essentials of a developmental mentoring relationship comes from an intranet site designed by my colleague Jenny Sweeney:

Mentoring is a partnership between two people built upon trust. It is a process in which the mentor offers ongoing support and development opportunities to the mentee. Addressing issues and blockages identified by the mentee, the mentor offers guidance, counselling and support in the form of pragmatic and objective assistance. Both share a common purpose of developing a strong two-way learning relationship.

Mentoring helps mentees and mentors progress their personal and professional growth. Its primary focus tends to be on the acquisition of people skills which enable individuals to operate effectively at high levels of management. The aim of mentoring is to build the capability of the mentees to the point of self-reliance while accelerating the communication of ideas across the organisation.

The mentoring relationship is confidential. The mentor offers a safe environment to the mentee within which they can discuss work-related issues and explore solutions to challenges. For this reason, in a formal mentoring scheme mentors are rarely in a line relationship; they are off-line. In this way, the mentors are not required to evaluate the current work performance of the mentees. They are there to help the learner manage his or her own learning.

Mentors can help individuals reach significant decisions about complex issues. Through skilful questioning they help clarify the mentee's perspective while bringing an additional view to bear on the issues. Mentors are not there to solve problems but rather to illuminate the issues and to help plan ways through them.

Mentoring is a positive developmental activity. Mentors can discuss current issues relating to the mentees' work, offering insights into the ways the organisation works, how the informal networks operate and how they think about the challenges and opportunities they encounter.

Mentors can advise on development and how to manage a career plan; they can challenge assumptions; and, where relevant, they can share their own experience. Mentoring has proved to be very effective in transferring tacit knowledge within an organisation, highlighting how effective people think, take decisions and approach complex issues.

Sharing views and ideas builds understanding and trust. The mentor and mentee relationship often evolves into a key friendship, invaluable when difficult decisions arise.

A SIMPLE MODEL OF DEVELOPMENTAL RELATIONSHIPS

Understanding the dynamics of mentoring relationships is not necessarily straightforward, as Figure 1 indicates. Every relationship operates within a context, which for formal mentoring involves the culture and/or climate of the organisation, the structure and purpose of the scheme, and the background of the mentor and mentee. Each mentoring pair brings to the relationship a set of expectations about the purpose of the relationship, about their role and the behaviours they should adopt, and about the likely outcomes. Many or all of these expectations will be influenced by the context. The interaction between the mentor and mentee is a self-reinforcing system – each party's behaviour influences the behaviour of the other. This in turn will influence the process – eg how frequently they meet, how deeply they explore issues. And finally, the effectiveness of the process will have a strong influence on the outcomes, which can be categorised as either supporting (often referred to in the literature as 'psychosocial') or career-oriented.

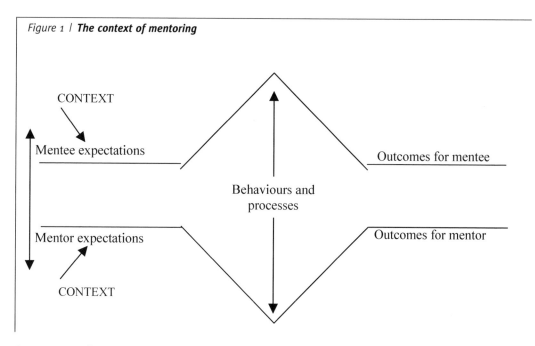

Figure 1 | *The context of mentoring*

Outcomes will normally need to be positive for both sides in order for the relationship to continue much beyond the short term. If either mentors or mentees feel that they are getting nothing for their efforts, the relationship will falter and die. The challenge is to provide ways of describing what we mean by mentoring that are both academically sound and simple for people to understand and apply. In this chapter we explore a basic model that fits those criteria, then some alternative perspectives on mentoring that help to distinguish it from other forms of helping others to learn and grow.

THE TWO DIMENSIONS OF 'HELPING TO LEARN'

The core model of mentoring – the dynamic that drives a high proportion of the schemes and programmes around the world outside the USA – derives from two key relationship variables.

The first of these is 'Who's in charge?'

If the mentor takes primary responsibility for managing the relationship (by deciding the content, timing and direction of discussion, by pointing the mentee towards specific career or personal goals, or by giving strong advice and suggestions), then the relationship is *directive* in tone. If he or she, by contrast, encourages the mentee to set the agenda and initiate meetings, encourages the mentee to come to his or her own conclusions about the way forward and generally stimulates the development of self-reliance, then the relationship is relatively *non-directive* (see Figure 2). Support for this dimension of helping behaviour comes from a variety of resources both within the mentoring literature and in the parallel literatures on counselling and coaching as well as interviewing and appraisal.

For example, Barham and Conway's (1998) study of the influence of cultural factors on mentor behaviour concludes that where managers expect their normal role to be that of expert,

The style of the mentoring relationship will be more didactic and less empowered from the mentee's perspective.

Where the culture expects managers to be facilitators, however,

The balance of the relationship will be more equal and it will be about mutual learning and sharing. There will be an empowered 'feel' to the mentoring relationships.

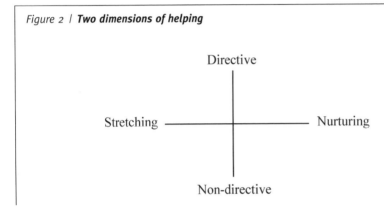

Figure 2 | **Two dimensions of helping**

Recent studies suggest strongly that the most effective relationships in which personal development is the desired outcome are those in which the mentee is relatively proactive and the mentor relatively passive or reactive. The opposite is probably true for relationships that are more focused on sponsorship behaviours.

The second dimension relates to the individual's need.

Is it primarily about learning – being challenged and stretched – or about nurturing – being supported and encouraged? Again, this is a dimension well established in the general psychological literature, and in particular that on leadership. Blake and Mouton (1964), Schriesheim and Murphy (1976), Likert (1961) and others emphasise the importance of both task orientation and consideration/social support in achieving group goals. The effective mentoring relationship similarly requires a mixture (often shifting with the needs of the mentee) of task-focus (for which read challenge or stretching) and supporting behaviours (for which read nurturing). Authors such as Darling (1984) refer to both types of behaviours in their descriptions of what mentors do.

The stretching/nurturing dimension also reflects the complex duality of the goddess Athena – the real mentor in the Greek myth. She is at the same time the macho, fearsome huntress and the nurturing Earth Mother. Athena, who was closely associated with the owl as a symbol of wisdom, was frequently depicted in full armour and even was supposed to have been born fully armed! Yet she was also closely associated with handicrafts and agriculture. It is tempting to view these as masculine/feminine characteristics, and some writers have done just that. However, in my experience this can all too easily lead people into styles of mentoring behaviour based on gender stereotypes. The essence of effective mentoring is that mentors have the facility to move along the dimensions, in any direction, in response to their observation of the learner's need at the time.

The beauty of this model is its combination of simplicity and inclusiveness. All 'helping to learn' behaviours fit within these broad dimensions. ('Teaching' is not necessarily a helping-to-learn behaviour *per se* – being taught is something that is done to you, whereas learning is something you do yourself, or with someone else.) We can isolate four primary 'helping to learn' styles based on the dimensions (see Figure 3), on which a fifth is based.

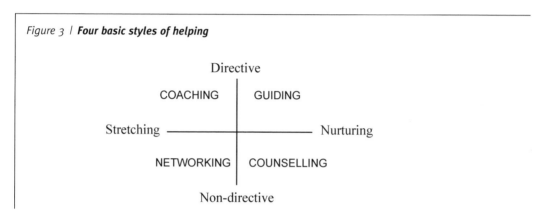

Figure 3 | *Four basic styles of helping*

Coaching

Coaching is a relatively directive means of helping someone develop competence. It is relatively directive because the coach is in charge of the process. Although there are, in turn, four basic styles of coaching, which range from the highly directive to more stimulative, learner-driven approaches, it is common for the learning goals to be set either by the coach or by a third party. In the world of work, coaching goals are most frequently established as an outcome of performance appraisal. The issue of learner commitment (is this really what matters to them?) is therefore relevant. Some of the useful behaviours effective coaches may display include challenging the learner's assumptions, being a critical friend and demonstrating how they do something the learner is having difficulties with.

Counselling

Counselling – in the context of support and learning, as opposed to therapy – is a relatively non-directive means of helping someone cope. By acting as a sounding-board, helping someone structure and analyse career-influencing decisions, and sometimes simply by being there to listen, the mentor supports the mentee in taking responsibility for his or her career and personal development.

Networking

To function effectively within any organisation, people need personal networks. At the very least they need an information network (how do I find out what I need to know?) and an influence network (how do I get people, over whom I have no direct control, to do things for me?). The same is true for the unemployed young adult in the context of community mentoring, for newly recruited researchers at university and for people in many other situations where mentoring can be applied. Effective mentors help their mentees develop self-resourcefulness by making them aware of the plethora of influence and information resources available to them – people, organisations and more formal repositories of knowledge. They may make an introduction to someone they already know, or talk the mentee through how he or she will make his or her own introduction to that person, or help the mentee build entire chunks of virgin network.

Guiding

Guiding (effectively acting as a guardian) is another relatively hands-on role and is the one most managers find easiest because it is closest to what they do normally. Giving advice comes naturally. It is unfortunate that so many managers who have attended coaching courses or read well-meant books on the developmental role of the supervisor come away feeling guilty, or worse, that they have to constantly restrain themselves from giving straight answers to their direct reports. The reality is that there are many situations where asking 'What do you think you should do?' is not an appropriate response. Using the tools of reflective analysis at inappropriate times is likely to have a far greater demotivating effect than simply leaving well alone. Equally, however, always providing the answer is not going to help someone grow. Because being a guide/guardian tends to carry with it a relatively strong element of being a role model – an example of success in whatever field the learner has chosen to pursue – one's behaviours, good or bad, are likely to be passed on to the learner along with more practical support. At an extreme, guide/guardians become sponsors or godfathers, taking a very direct interest in the learner's development, putting the learner forward for high-profile tasks, tipping him or her off about opportunities and actively moulding the learner's career. This can be very stifling for the recipient, who may not be in a position to resist this largesse should the learner prefer to succeed by his or her own resources. If learners comply with the mentors' manipulations, a subtle psychological contract often emerges in which career progression is traded for loyalty and respect. Some cultures regard this more positively than others.

Mentoring

Finally, mentoring draws on all four other 'helping to learn' styles. Indeed, the core skill of a mentor can be described as having sufficient sensitivity to the mentee's needs to respond with the appropriate behaviours. Thus, the effective mentor may use the challenging behaviours of stretch coaching at one point and the empathetic listening of counselling a short while later.

Where an organisation, or a national culture, or a mentoring pair, decide to draw the boundaries of what is appropriate behaviour for a mentor may vary substantially. What we call developmental mentoring assumes a diamond across the middle of the diagram (Figure

4). Traditional US mentoring, by contrast, is concentrated on a circle centred in the top right-hand corner (Figure 5), and often encompasses a high level of sponsoring behaviours.

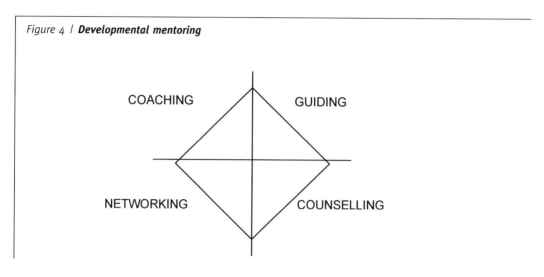

Figure 4 | Developmental mentoring

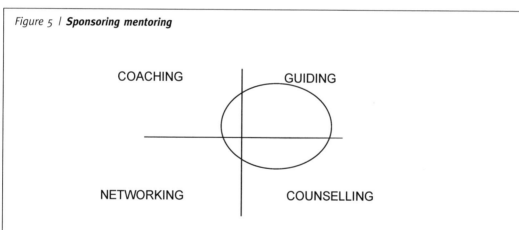

Figure 5 | Sponsoring mentoring

Table 1 (next page) explains the distinction between developmental and sponsoring mentoring in more detail. Essentially, one emphasises empowerment and personal account-ability; the other the effective use of power and influence.

Table 1 | **Developmental v sponsoring mentoring: the fundamental differences**

Developmental mentoring	Sponsoring mentoring
Mentee (literally, one who is helped to think)	Protégé (literally, one who is protected
Two-way learning	One-way learning
The power and authority of the mentor are 'parked'	The mentor's power to influence is central to the relationship
Mentor helps mentee decide what he/she wants and plan how to achieve it	Mentor intervenes on mentee's behalf
Begins with an ending in mind	Often ends in conflict, when mentee outgrows mentor and rejects advice
Built on learning opportunities and friendship	Built on reciprocal loyalty
Most common form of help is stimulating insight	Most common forms of help are advice and introductions
Mentor may be peer or even junior – it is experience that counts	Mentor is older and more senior

MENTORING AS REFLECTIVE SPACE

On average, knowledge workers cannot usefully obtain more than 10 minutes at a time to focus without interruption on a specific task or issue. Although people are often working longer hours than a decade ago, they have less and less time to stop and think deeply. In experiments with hundreds of managers and professionals, fewer than 3 per cent claim to find their deep thinking time at work, and of these, the majority do so by coming in very early in the morning. For most people, however, deep thinking time happens on the journey to and from work, in the bath or shower, taking exercise, doing the ironing, lying awake at night, or in other parts of their 'free' time.

Deep, reflective thinking is as essential to the effectiveness of our conscious brain as REM sleep is to our unconscious. In both cases we become dysfunctional if our minds do not carry out the essential task of analysing, structuring, organising and storing. When we allow ourselves to enter personal reflective space (PRS), we put the world around us largely on hold. (Even if we are doing a complex physical movement, like jogging, or driving the car, we allow our internal autopilot to take over.) Often unbidden, although with practice it is possible to control the process, one issue of concern rises to the surface of our consciousness and we start to examine it with a depth and clarity we have not previously been able to apply to it. There are many comparisons for this process – I like the analogy of the mine disposal engineer gingerly examining a sea mine washed ashore.

Another analogy is peering through the windows of a doll's house before gradually disassembling it.

Whatever metaphor you use, the process is the same: you ask yourself questions about the issue in an attempt to better understand it and its impact on you. The more questions you ask from different perspectives, the more likely you are to achieve some level of insight which allows you to position the issue very differently and consider new ways of dealing with it. For me, a remarkably high proportion of excursions into reflective space result in being able to combine two difficult and until then separate situations in a way that achieves a positive outcome for both. Some people find that PRS takes them to a better understanding of the dynamics of their situation and gives them the confidence to take actions they had been avoiding. Possibly everyone is different, but there are at least two factors common to everyone who enters PRS regularly:

- He or she emerges with renewed energy to tackle the issue he or she has been considering.

- Whether vocalised or not, the person has been having a dialogue with himself or herself. (This is not a sign of madness, I hasten to add.)

When you engage in similar dialogue with a mentor, you are in effect inviting him or her to join you in your PRS. The dialogue becomes a trialogue, the mentor asking you similar questions, but more rigorously, more objectively, from a wider range of perspectives, and more intensively. The effective mentor therefore takes you down the path from analysis, through understanding and insight, to plans for action in a faster, more thorough manner.

An example

The owner/manager of a 65-employee company was forced by a minor but significant health warning to consider throttling back on his hours and responsibilities. He was frustrated, however, by a complete failure to delegate key tasks to his three direct reports. After a while he gave up – until the next heart twinge brought the issue back to the fore. This time he sought help, asking a mentor to help him think the issues through. The mentor asked the kinds of question that put the behaviours of both sides into perspective – a set of unconscious collusions that would always result in problems being passed up to the boss. Whatever the conscious expectations the owner and his managers had of each other, the unconscious ones were those driving both sides' behaviour. Teasing these expectations into the open allowed the owner to design and implement a whole new range of tactics, which broke the fixed, negative cycle of behaviour and changed the relationship with two out of the three managers. (You can't win all the time!) One solution was to stop getting angry when the managers asked him to take a decision within their authority. Instead, he now patiently explained what they should do. When they arrived back at their offices, however, they found an invoice 'For doing your job' and an appropriate sum deducted from their departmental budgets!

MENTORING IN THE SPECTRUM OF LEARNING

People learn from others in a variety of ways, and one sign of learning maturity is that a person has a wide network of different learning relationships. In many ways, the journey to adulthood is one of widening one's range of learning relationships.

*Table 2 | **Key differences in style when helping others to learn***

Role	Relation-ship	Dominant style	Affinity	Learning transfer	Power management
Teacher	Pupil	Tell	Aloof	Explicit data and information	High exerted power (parental)
Tutor	Student	Discuss		Knowledge	
Coach	Learner	Demonstrate/ give feedback		Skills	
Mentor	Colleague	Encourage/ stimulate	Close	Intuitive data and wisdom	Low exerted power (collegial)

First, really good teachers are able to operate across the spectrum, although the structure and organisation of modern school systems makes it increasingly difficult for them to do so. Second, each of these approaches is both valid and valuable, but they represent a spectrum from the highly impersonal to the highly customised and personal. Third, one can also plot an evolution in the quality of the learning, in two ways. One is that the closer one gets to mentoring, the more the learning is shaped and encapsulated by the individual's own experiences. The other is the cascade from data through information (a product of teaching), knowledge (tutoring), and skills (coaching) to wisdom (mentoring). At each stage of this cascade the level of usefulness increases: data becomes interesting (except to train-spotters) only when it is organised into information; information allows people to pass examinations, but it requires further structure and context to turn it into knowledge, at which point it can be applied more widely. Having the knowledge of what a good manager should do does not mean that you are any good at it, however. For that, knowledge has to be applied and re-applied until it becomes skill. Finally, wisdom is the ability to apply accumulated knowledge and skills more widely again, having the judgement to draw meaningfully on experience in one or more situations in completely new contexts.

The implications of this for mentors are considerable. Whose wisdom are we talking about? Effective mentors tend to treat their wisdom like a nuclear arsenal – they very rarely let it fly. Instead they use their experience to inform the questions they ask and to challenge assumptions the mentee may be making. They also recognise that the greatest value to the mentee is to develop his or her own wisdom, not to borrow that of the mentor. Inevitably, in a successful and enduring mentoring relationship there will be nuggets of observations by the mentor that the mentee will savour and perhaps pass on in turn, but the prevailing message of developmental mentoring is, 'Look into your own experience. Learn your own lessons. Build your own wisdom.' (This is heavily in contrast with the sponsorship mentoring view of 'Listen to my experience. Learn from my triumphs and mistakes. Value my advice and judgement.')

COACHING *V* MENTORING

Given the frequent confusion between these two terms, it is worth drawing out the differences more finely. Although coaching and mentoring share some tools and approaches, coaching is primarily focused on performance within the current job and emphasises the development of skills. Mentoring is primarily focused on longer-term goals and on developing capability. Table 3 puts more flesh on these bones.

*Table 3 | **Coaching contrasted with mentoring***

Coaching	Mentoring
Concerned with task	Concerned with implications beyond the task
Focuses on skills and performances	Focuses on capability and potential
Primarily a line manager role	Works best off-line
Agenda set by or with the coach	Agenda set by the learner
Emphasises feedback to the learner	Emphasises feedback and reflection by the learner
Typically addresses a short-term need	Typically a longer-term relationship, often 'for life'
Feedback and discussion primarily explicit	Feedback and discussion primarily about implicit, intuitive issues and behaviours

There are four basic styles of coaching, which can be reduced at their basic to

- tell,
- show,
- suggest, and
- stimulate.

The most common style in the workplace is *tell*, in which the coach agrees with the learner a task and an expected level of performance, allows him or her to do the task, then gives him or her constructive feedback and helps him or her to plan how to do better next time. This is territory not shared with mentoring. Another unshared territory, generally speaking, is the *show* style, in which the coach demonstrates how to do a task, then asks the learner to copy what he or she has seen, after which both discuss what happened. The closest a mentor may get to this style is to invite the learner to collaborate on a task so that the learner can observe, ask questions and develop his or her own approaches.

The *suggest* style can be compatible with mentoring. The coach effectively says, 'When you do this task, think about the following things ...', and so focuses attention on particular aspects he or she thinks will be helpful. For a mentor, this would be akin to giving targeted advice. The emphasis of feedback here has shifted from the extrinsic (provided for the learner) to the intrinsic (provided by the learner himself or herself).

Where coaching and mentoring are fully aligned, however, is in the *stimulate* style, which is basically about helping people think things through for themselves, through dialogue that encourages self-analysis, reflection and intrinsic feedback. This implies more emphasis on questioning than advising.

MENTORING IN THE SPECTRUM OF SUPPORTING

In that mentoring – and all other developmental styles – addresses needs for both learning/stretching and support/nurturing, it is not surprising that we can identify a similar hierarchy of supporting roles and behaviours. The most directive or hands-on role is that of sponsor. Figure 6 draws out the main differences between sponsorship and mentoring.

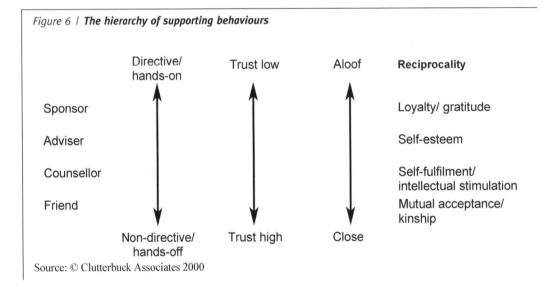

*Figure 6 | **The hierarchy of supporting behaviours***

Source: © Clutterbuck Associates 2000

Giving advice is a key supporting role, especially for those occasions when the learner simply does not know what to do or how to move forward on an issue. Sometimes the adviser is simply a sounding-board. Being sought out for one's knowledge or insight is one of the strongest compliments a person can receive – it raises one's self-esteem and encourages future helpfulness.

Being a counsellor is in may ways similar, but the satisfaction comes from the use of one's knowledge and skills to help someone reach his or her own conclusions and solve his or her own problems. The counsellor is also much more likely than the adviser to reflect on how the issues considered relate to himself or herself and his or her own circumstances.

Friendship is the least directive of roles and the one – in its most beneficial manifestations – that demands least from the participants. Friends may sometimes act in the other supporting roles, where circumstances make it appropriate. Critical friends are a valuable source of feedback, which the individual might not otherwise receive.

Mentors might adopt any or all of these roles, depending on the style of mentoring agreed. A traditional US approach would place more emphasis on sponsoring and advising; a developmental mentoring approach would avoid sponsoring and would concentrate on a mixture of advising and counselling behaviours. Either model of mentoring could result in the development of friendship, but friendships tend to be deeper and longer-lasting in developmental mentoring, perhaps because both parties in successful relationships learn to be very open with each other.

There are, however, many similarities between coaching and mentoring in terms of the behaviours applied. The effective mentor has a wider repertoire because he or she also draws on behaviours and techniques shared with counselling, guiding/guardianship and network development. In practice many companies, such as BAT, use mentoring and coaching as mutually reinforcing roles, and this seems to bring out the best in both. In BAT's case, graduate recruits have a series of coaches who are their immediate line managers as they move around the organisation, gathering breadth of experience in their first two years. They also have a mentor who is off-line and has a wider, more pastoral role and with whom they can discuss their progression beyond the current job assignments.

Other organisations have recognised that high-flyers need a portfolio of relationships. In particular, they benefit from having:

- a coach, to focus upon performance issues, especially for the current job role

- a mentor, to challenge them, provide the bigger picture and concentrate on longer-term development

- a sponsor, to ensure that they are placed in the right assignments to develop their potential

- peer learning relationships, both within and across the organisational boundaries

- access to traditional learning resources, such as business school courses, and new media, such as e-learning, at times when they have a specific learning need.

Integrating these roles could present a challenge, but most senior managers in an organisation seem perfectly capable of managing their learning portfolio without problem.

SUMMARY

This has been a very short introduction to fundamental but relatively straightforward ways of thinking about and describing the mentoring phenomenon. There are other descriptive models well worth a look – in particular, Carter and Levis's (1994) notion of mentoring contexts – and some of these are to be found in the recommended further reading in the Bibliography. From my experience, however, the three models described in this chapter provide a very effective means of focusing both mentor and mentee on pragmatic expectations, both of each other and of the mentoring process.

3

How formal should the mentoring programme be?

Not long ago, a petrochemicals company asked me to examine its two pilot, high-profile mentoring schemes – why were they not working? Although launched with great enthusiasm and a considerable effort to train mentors, many of the relationships had simply never taken off. Others had faded away, often because the pair had run out of interesting things to talk about.

The problems stemmed from a variety of failings, not least insufficient clarity about roles and objectives. However, one of the most interesting results of our analysis of data gathered through focus groups was that the relationships that worked best and most often were generally those where the mentees themselves selected their mentors.

Those relationships where the mentors were effectively imposed by the organisation were less effective and less likely to continue. This distinction was particularly marked among a group of high-flyers who had one mentor of each kind – the allocated mentor being from the same general area of the business and the personally selected mentor coming from another department. Yet I know from experiences in other companies that encouraging people to select mentors entirely at their own choice leads in a high proportion of cases to relationships that deliver few, if any, benefits. Left to their own devices, people often choose someone they get on with extremely well and have known for a long time, or they approach a more senior high-flyer with a view to hanging on to their coat-tails. In the first case, although there is good rapport, there is typically very little opportunity for learning – growing pearls of learning requires at least some measure of grit in the oyster. When the chosen mentor is a high-flyer, he or she is often uninterested in helping to develop others – even if the high-flyer is interested, he or she is unable to create the necessary time.

It is as a result of this kind of contradiction in experience that emerging best practice in dealing with selection and matching centres on 'guided choice'. This can mean providing the mentee with strong guidance on how to find and use a mentor, or it can involve giving a limited number of options, selected by the scheme co-ordinator against criteria that the mentee has provided or at least been involved in. The second of these approaches requires an existing pool of people who have volunteered and ideally been trained to be mentors.

There is, however, an even bigger conflict about mentoring, which is starting to be resolved and to which I referred in passing in Chapter 2. Put briefly, although most practitioners –

both in-company and consultants – maintain that formal mentoring (ie a structured programme in which mentoring relationships are established and supported) is far more effective than informal, most academics, particularly in the USA, say that their studies show the opposite to be true. The clash between scientific observation and the experience of practitioners is not unique to mentoring – it happens in almost every aspect of endeavour – but understanding the reasons for the differences almost always stimulates a leap forward in practical implementation. And that is what is beginning to happen in mentoring right now.

THE ARGUMENTS FOR FORMAL MENTORING

Social inclusion

The main arguments in favour of a formal structure for mentoring centre on the need for some control of a process that, left alone, may not always work to the advantage of the organisation or the majority of the people in it. Social inclusion is an issue of increasing importance in most large organisations – how do we ensure both equal opportunities and the effective use of the diversity of talent, experience and backgrounds of our people? There are many well-documented cases of programmes aimed at a specific group that break the glass ceilings in gender, race or disability. The Cabinet Office, for example, runs a highly successful mentoring scheme aimed at people with severe physical (and sometimes mental) disability who have ambitions to progress. The mentors are all very senior Civil Servants who see the relationship as a stimulating challenge. Some of the most dramatic figures on mentoring for social inclusion come from the programme Big Brothers/Big Sisters, which links young people at risk in North America (and more recently in the UK) with a mentor in the community. The 10–16-year-old mentees in this programme are:

- 46 per cent less likely to begin drug abuse (70 per cent for minorities)
- 27 per cent less likely to begin underage drinking
- 30 per cent less likely to hit someone else.

They also skip 80 per cent fewer schooldays than non-mentored peers and have better relationships with parents, peers and teachers.

By contrast, informal mentoring appears to reinforce social exclusion because the scarce pool of mentors tends to be snapped up by those who are from the dominant social group, who are better educated and more obviously ambitious. In Europe and North America, this means that white male graduates are far more likely to find an informal mentor than any other group. Because mentor and mentee are so similar, an additional negative is that relatively little learning takes place on the part of the mentor. Diversity in a mentoring relationship stimulates examining issues from different perspectives.

Positive mentoring

Formal mentoring also helps ensure that the relationship has clear purpose. The most common reason that so many mentoring relationships fail is that neither mentor nor mentee is quite sure what he or she is aiming for, so there is no sense of direction. A formal scheme provides an umbrella purpose for the organisation, which helps mentor and mentee establish more specific goals for their own relationship. Formal mentoring also ensures that there is a practical framework of support for mentor and mentee, including initial training and, in good practice environments, some form of continuing review by which mentors can address any further skills needs they identify. Training ensures that both parties understand what is expected of them – not least who manages the relationship and what the boundaries are. The formal process also helps to weed out 'toxic' mentors. People who have manipulative goals, who represent values the organisation is trying to move away from, or who have so many problems of their own that they end up transferring these to the mentee are all common characters who can damage both the mentee and the organisation and who may actively seek to find mentees in an informal environment.

THE ARGUMENTS FOR INFORMAL MENTORING

A variety of highly analytical studies, mostly in the USA, suggest that people in informal mentoring relationships are much more satisfied with them. Among the reasons suggested for this are:

- Informal relationships take longer to get off the ground and tend to last longer overall, so there is more opportunity to create strong trust and to achieve medium-term goals. Formal relationships are often under considerable time pressure. Informal mentors are less likely to be in the role out of some form of obligation; they are there because they want to be. (There is evidence that altruistic mentors are less effective than those who see benefits for themselves in the relationship.) Many companies with formal schemes put subtle pressure on managers to become mentors as a way to demonstrate their commitment to people development.

- Informal mentors tend to have better communication and coaching skills than formal. (This is a matter of numbers – formal schemes often create increased demand that can be filled only by relaxing the competence criteria. In informal mentoring, the people most likely to put themselves forward – toxic mentors excepted – are those who have confidence in their own competence to perform the role.)

Broadly, these studies suggest that informal mentors offer stronger elements of friendship and empathy than formal mentors. Most of the other differences identified relate to the mentor's willingness to act as a sponsor to the mentee – something seen as positive in traditional US mentoring but as a practice to avoid in European developmental mentoring, which places much more emphasis on helping the mentee become more self-resourceful.

SUMMARY

Getting the best from a mentoring scheme, then, involves building in the best aspects of both formal and informal approaches. A formal structure is essential because it provides meaning and direction for relationships and support where necessary. But individual relationships will flourish best when allowed to operate as informally as possible. Successful formal relationships very frequently go on to become successful informal ones. There is also an increasing body of field evidence that the quality and extent of informal mentoring improves dramatically once a critical mass is achieved of people who have been effective mentors and mentees under formal arrangements. An organisation that manages to create a mentoring/coaching culture can increasingly relax the level of formal intervention it imposes. What structures it does provide – in terms of educational materials and training, for example – become regarded as support mechanisms rather than as controls. Meetings between mentors to develop their skills can become informal, self-driven support networks. And the range of people from whom the mentees learn can gradually be extended as they learn to build and manage their own learning nets.

4

Making the case for mentoring

Like all developmental interventions, making the case for investment in mentoring is not necessarily straightforward. The chain of cause and effect may be distorted, especially if the mentoring programme is just one part of a larger initiative or package of initiatives – for example, as one of a number of support measures for promoting diversity, or as part of a graduate induction programme.

Nonetheless, there are sufficient cases of very specific benefit from mentoring programmes and relationships to produce a very strong case to all four of the key internal audiences:

- top management
- prospective mentees
- prospective mentors, and
- key third parties such as line managers.

For all of these, the two basic questions are: How do I know the investment (of time, energy and/or money) is worthwhile? Why do I need to invest in a formal support structure or relationship, rather than let mentoring happen naturally and informally?

THE CASE TO TOP MANAGEMENT

Every company needs some form of career development programme to produce a succession of motivated, upward-moving employees. Even employees who are destined to remain at the same level may need career development as the jobs they are in change or become obsolete. Managers with high potential should identify and improve their skills, set career goals and know how to achieve those goals in the most practical and efficient way. Conventional career development courses provide some of the answers, but all too often fail to provide adequate follow-up. The results, too, are often hard to define. Schemes involving selection by assessment centres of high-flyers or frequent job rotation to gain wide experience probably offer the nearest thing to tangible results, but are extremely expensive, not least because at each change the young person has to start again at the beginning of the learning cycle of the new job.

Leaving career development solely to managers, although cheaper, tends to be singularly ineffective. A manager may lack the ability to recognise a potential high-flyer or, if he or she does, be reluctant to lose that employee by counselling him or her to move to another area of the company. Managers who are unavailable, uncommitted, or who dislike particular subordinates can effectively block the career paths of talented employees and prevent them from realising their potential. Diversity objectives also tend to be marginalised, unless there is a structured programme to promote and monitor them.

A mentoring programme, as a formal method of recognising talent in a company, is a viable alternative to both these approaches. It can be carried out in tandem with traditional career development methods and has reasonably good predictability in its results. It may be run for as long as the employee benefits from it. As in many other relationships, both mentee and mentor have to work hard to make it succeed; both can draw substantial benefits.

Mentoring can work in most organisations, regardless of size, culture or market sector. It can communicate to employees far more fully the complexity of procedures and the unique nature of the company than any formal training course, induction booklets or company manual.

Mentoring enhances the abilities of both the mentor and mentee, so the organisation gains through increased efficiency. Companies with formal, longstanding mentoring programmes claim tangible increases in productivity and efficiency. Intangible benefits include improved staff morale, greater career satisfaction and swifter getting up to speed when mentored managers are inserted into a new job.

Another significant impetus behind mentoring is the cost – not in cash terms (mentoring is not a cheap alternative when you take into account the value of management time) – but in saving on expensive off-site courses which take employees away from productive activity for weeks on end.

The primary rewards to a company of a mentoring programme are:

- easier recruitment and induction
- improved employee motivation
- the management of the corporate culture
- succession planning
- improved communications
- staff retention.

Easier recruitment and induction

A formal mentoring programme eases the sometimes difficult process of assimilating new recruits. Companies such as BAe Systems and National Grid, for example, have found graduate induction has become less of an ordeal since they began mentoring. Enthusiasm has been productively channelled, and graduates are taking on greater responsibility as their commitment grows.

Most staff turnover occurs during the first six to 12 months with a new employer, and a major cause is inability to adjust rapidly enough. Assigning a mentor to a new arrival helps overcome the counterproductive problems of culture shock and the uncertainty most people feel as they find their feet in the new environment. Employees become productive more quickly and are likely to stay with the company longer.

Mentoring also cultivates in the mentee an increased sense of commitment and loyalty to the organisation. The mentor is the mediator between the mentee and the company. Through close interaction with the mentee, the mentor creates a personal atmosphere in what might otherwise seem a faceless bureaucratic organisation. The mentee receives through the mentor a positive perception of the company. The mentee can be made to feel that he or she is participating in the inner operations of the company, and this in turn generates a closer identification with the organisation's goals.

Many companies experience difficulties in attracting the right kind of graduates, even in times of severe unemployment. Even top financial services companies in the City of London are finding that graduates – and especially those with advanced degrees – turn down employers who do not offer a mentoring programme. A mentoring programme can be a significant inducement for graduates to join less glamorous firms or industries because it demonstrates commitment to management development and staff retention. It is particularly attractive if it offers a fast track to middle management.

Improved employee motivation

Mentoring can help reduce managerial and professional turnover at other critical stages, too. Young, ambitious people often undergo a period of frustration and impatience when they realise their progress up the company career ladder is slower than they initially expected. If mentees have a mentor who is taking an active interest in their career and who explains the reasons for and ways round current blockages, they are more likely to persevere. The mentor helps them understand and recognise the long-term plans the company has for them, and helps the mentee make the most of the learning experiences inherent in the current job. In this way mentoring lessens the threat that other companies may lure away promising young employees with offers of speedier career advancement.

A mentoring relationship also motivates the middle and senior managers involved and can be a valuable means of delaying 'plateauing'. A manager is less likely to retire mentally in the job if he or she is constantly faced with fresh challenges arising from a mentoring relationship. Mentors are forced to clarify and articulate their own ideas about the company's organisation and goals in order to explain them to their mentees. They may feel they have to improve their own abilities to justify the mentees' respect. Cultivating potential in the company becomes a significant opportunity for the mentor to demonstrate that the old dog is still capable of learning and showing new tricks. As a result, mentors may find new purpose and interest in their jobs.

The management of the corporate culture

In the original edition I titled this section 'A stable corporate culture'. Almost every mentoring programme I examined then had as part of its objectives passing on the nuances of the corporate culture. In the intervening years the emphasis has changed dramatically. Instead of preserving cultures, companies are desperately trying to change them. This poses a number of problems – not least that it makes it even more difficult to identify mentors with the 'right' values.

Mentor and mentee in an effective developmental relationship are able to explore the differences between espoused corporate values and actual behaviour. At the same time, the mentor helps to clarify in the mentee's mind which aspects of the culture are fixed and not open to challenge, and which are open for dialogue. At one of the world's largest and most successful merchant banks, for example, new recruits soon learn that near-obsessive honesty is an immutable part of the culture, but that maintaining a work-life balance (on a par with integrity in the corporate values statement) is honoured more often in the breach. The mentee is able to use the mentor as a role model for selected aspects of the culture, while the mentor is able to use the mentee's constructive challenge to inform the continuing senior-level debate on how the culture should evolve.

Bringing mentors together from time to time to continue their skills development and review relationship progress (within the bounds of confidentiality) has proved valuable in changing how the organisation tackles important issues relating to culture.

For example: an international IT services company held as a basic assumption about how people's careers should evolve that they should move as early as possible into positions of junior supervision and thence to manage small projects, until they began to climb the management ladder. The mentors revealed, however, that a significant proportion of the workforce just wanted to become better and better techies. One of the main reasons talent was leaving the company was that these people felt the culture was incompatible with their needs. The result was that the company introduced a dual-path career system.

A financial services company had stifled discussion about work-life balance issues for years. With the introduction of a mentoring programme, people had an opportunity to open up about their anger in respect of the long hours culture. Suddenly, top management could no longer pretend the problem did not exist, and it committed to making changes happen.

Succession planning

An increasingly common benefit reported by larger companies is an improvement in succession planning. Widespread mentoring, especially where the duration of formal relationships is limited to one or two years, ensures that senior managers are familiar with the strengths, weaknesses and ambitions of a relatively large pool of more junior talent.

Improved communications

In a traditional senior to junior mentoring relationship, the mentee's unique position in the organisation can aid informal communications because he or she straddles several levels. For example, through the relationship with the mentor the junior management mentee has access to and is accepted by middle management. At the same time he or she is accepted in the lower managerial levels. Because the mentee is familiar with the language and mannerisms of both, he or she can efficiently communicate each group's ideas and opinions to the other. Rich informal communication networks improve productivity and efficiency in a company since they lead to more action, more innovation, more learning, and swifter adjustment to changing business needs.

It can be lonely at the top. The chance to pass information to lower levels of management restores interdependence between management levels and eases the flow of ideas and information. This special communications network also facilitates easier working of other areas of management development.

Improved communications between headquarters and the field has been a significant result in a number of mentoring schemes. In one UK public sector organisation, headquarters was trying to rein in the regional barons, who had virtually declared independence and who actively discouraged their people from getting too close to headquarters employees. Headquarters had at the same time allowed itself to become somewhat aloof and disconnected. Deliberately pairing mentors and mentees across this divide increased understanding and established a quality of dialogue that overcame most of the hostilities.

Mentoring can sometimes benefit an organisation in unexpected ways, too. In one company a mentee was being mentored with the ultimate objective of helping him leave. A spokesman explained:

> *This highly talented individual has gone as far as is possible in this company. We have no appropriate position for him, so we are grooming him to take over a small corporation outside this company. In the meantime, for the three to five years that he stays with us, we benefit from his productivity and enthusiasm. In the future we will have a very useful ally.*

A similar case arose in the north-west region of ICI's engineering department. The company explains:

> *A sponsored mechanical engineering student began training with us and met her mentor for about three hours on her first day. Two weeks later, she left us and decided to go up to university, forsaking her engineering ambitions. During this time the mentor had provided support, primarily in a counselling mode, to a person living away from home for the first time, in a strange environment. He helped her rethink her ambitions and come to a decision on her future.*

The most recent large-scale study of mentoring programmes in the UK (Industrial Society, 1995) found that the most common intention behind introducing a mentoring programme was to provide help and encouragement for those taking qualifications (56 per cent), followed by familiarising new recruits with the organisation (50 per cent), 'providing growth for any employee who requests a mentor' (46 per cent), developing senior managers (31 per cent) and fast-tracking (31 per cent). A handful of schemes addressed issues of equal opportunities.

Another study, this time from North America (CMSI, 2001), asked programme co-ordinators how satisfied they were with the return on investment from mentoring. Some 52 per cent said they were moderately satisfied, and 29 per cent said they were highly satisfied.

Improved retention of employees

Keeping the good people you have is increasingly being regarded as a core competitive advantage. In the war for talent, any reduction in employee turnover is a major benefit – and mentoring has been shown to play a major positive role in retention.

A key indicator is 'intention to quit'. US studies of employees in large companies indicate that 35 per cent are thinking of leaving within the next 12 months. However, among those who have a mentor, the figure falls to 16 per cent. When it comes to actual resignations, the figures are even more startling. In the finance division of SmithKline Beecham (now GlaxoSmithKline), staff turnover in 1999 was 27 per cent – except among people who had a mentor, where it was 2 per cent! Some allowance must be made in these figures for sample bias (people who have given up on the company are unlikely to seek a mentor within it), but that is likely only to have had a minor effect.

Similarly, Allied Irish Banks was losing a quarter of its annual intake of 200 graduates within the first 12 months each year. The only change made to the recruitment and induction programme was to introduce a mentoring process. The turnover rate dropped from 25 per cent to 8 per cent.

With graduates, opportunity to improve retention appears to lie in the transition period between the end of their formal induction and getting settled into their first supervisory job. Many mentoring schemes stopped when the graduate induction stopped. Good practice now seems to be to carry on for six months plus, to bridge this period of uncertainty and relatively low self-confidence.

Surveys in a number of countries indicate that people, who are in a mentoring relationship, are less than half as likely to be thinking of changing employers.

Other organisational benefits

The benefits described thus far are relatively generic, but in most cases organisations will have very specific goals for introducing and maintaining a mentoring programme. For example, a firm may have a very strong need to tackle diversity issues by opening up access to disadvantaged groups. Or it may wish to deal with the problems of stress and absenteeism by providing a safety valve for people's concerns. Other goals have included:

- helping 'invisible' people in finance become better known and demonstrate their abilities
- supporting managers in a bureaucratic culture to become more commercially minded
- establishing a professional development network for members of an engineering association
- helping entrepreneurs grow their management abilities in line with the demands of their businesses
- raising overall appraisal scores across a division

- helping new project teams gel more rapidly, so they can achieve the assigned task ahead of the competition

- increasing creativity and the quality of risk-taking.

Community organisations will have different goals again – from helping young people stay at school to helping the long-term unemployed find permanent work. The one common factor we can find across all the goals of successful mentoring programmes is that they aim to achieve an important organisational objective by assisting people to achieve their potential.

CALCULATING THE COST-BENEFIT OF MENTORING

Because most of the organisational benefits of mentoring are difficult to measure in cash terms, it is not easy to develop a convincing financial case other than for mentoring's effect on retention. A typical calculation for the latter might be:

The average cost of losing a skilled employee:

Recruiting a replacement (25% of salary)	£7,000
Work not delivered during the gap between departure of one and arrival/getting into harness of the other	£7,000
Loss of customers	£10,000
Training the new recruit to the same standard	£5,000
Total	£29,000

Clearly, the more senior and/or more critical the employee is to the company, the greater the cost.

Average cost per employee lost (A) multiplied by the number of employees lost each year provides a baseline cost of failure to retain. The minimum expected impact on those covered by the proposed programme is 25 per cent additional retention (B). The minimum net saving to the organisation is therefore A times B. The larger the programme, the higher the overall saving.

An additional direct saving relates to re-recruitment costs. HR can (and probably should) track the volume of employees returning to the organisation, and the proportion of these who are doing so because they maintained a positive relationship with a former mentor. Some mentoring programmes aimed at specific groups, such as mothers returning from maternity leave, are particularly straightforward to measure in this regard.

The more mentoring can be tied to clearly defined business goals, the easier it is to make a financial case. Connections that have been made by programme co-ordinators include:

- the cost of senior management and HR time in dealing with employee tribunals related to equal opportunity issues

- the cost of 'doing the milk round' versus that of having highly suitable graduates approaching the company (because of the reputation of its initial training, which includes mentoring) increased sales from newly appointed insurance agents

(20 per cent higher during their first year with the company)

- reduced costs of managing succession planning, because movement of talent is mainly within the company rather than out of it
- (for e-mentoring) reduced travel costs compared to classroom training.

In general, however, the financial case is not what swings the argument for or against mentoring. The top team either accepts that there is a wide range of mostly intangible but highly valuable benefits from mentoring, or it does not. If it does not, then it often makes sense to begin their education about the value of informal learning by concentrating on coaching, both in the line and – where accepted – externally for the leaders themselves. The more comfortable they become with performance-based task-oriented informal learning, the easier it becomes to make the step to understanding and valuing the more holistic learning of mentoring.

THE CASE TO THE MENTEE

Most of the early literature on mentoring assumed that the beneficiary would normally be a career-minded graduate with ambition and a desire to tap into the power sources of the organisation. The reality, of course, is that mentees come from a wide range of circumstances and that the benefits they seek are equally diverse.

Among the most common benefits are:

- obtaining opportunities to network and advice on how to grow your networks
- having available someone sympathetic who will understand difficult situations and help you work your way through them
- having someone to believe in you and your ability
- being given help to work out what you want from your life and work, and how to make the appropriate choices and sacrifices
- being given help in developing greater confidence
- working through tactics to manage relationships with other people
- becoming more comfortable in dealing with people from unfamiliar backgrounds
- making sense of feedback from other sources – putting it into context and deciding how to deal with it
- being given an opportunity to challenge the organisation's thinking and be challenged in one's own.

Although promotion to a more senior level is often a goal for the mentee, for many people the aim is to develop as a person and open up wider possibilities.

For example, Liz sought a mentor to help her through the transition from full-time employment with a construction company to being a self-employed consultant. She sought from the mentor reassurance that she had the capability to fulfil the new role, and assistance in planning how to make the switch in career. Hal, by contrast, wanted to stay in the same company but become more effective in integrating his work and non-work lives. (In practice, he did not have much of a life outside work.) For him, the mentor was someone who gave him permission to let go of responsibilities – even though, as someone outside the company, the mentor had no formal authority to do so. The mentor also provided a resource to whom Hal could talk when he found the going difficult.

Easier induction for those coming straight from university or moving to a new country

One mentor comments:

> *Mentoring is a means of smoothing out graduates' transition from an educational environment – one of the major changes of their life – and enabling them to settle in more quickly.*

According to the NHS in Wales, it 'provides exceptional opportunities and the unique status of having someone to trust in a bewildering environment', who can direct the mentee's learning opportunities.

A French mentee working in England stresses how important her mentor has been:

> *My mentor has worked abroad and can speak French. He has helped me to adapt to the British way of life. The scheme has definitely helped me to settle into this country and the company.*

Chemical company Hoechst had a dozen or so British apprentices in its German operations. Although they had a tutor in the UK, they also assigned German mentors to relieve isolation and to provide career counselling.

The same principle can be applied at a much more senior level – expatriate managers taking on roles in a new country need to learn the business and social culture rapidly. Having a local person, perhaps from another company, helping them through this transition is often greatly valued.

Improved self-confidence

The mentee gains a sense of self-worth and importance. The one-to-one relationship between the mentor and the mentee helps the latter feel that the company values him or her as an individual rather than as a cog in the managerial wheel. A mentor gives mentees (in particular, graduates) undergoing frequent job rotation and management change a point of stability in what may seem an unpredictable environment. By helping them explore their own potential, the mentor also enables them to gain the self-knowledge necessary for well-founded self-confidence.

Learning to cope with the formal and informal structure of the company

Through the mentor, the mentee learns about the formal culture of an organisation, its values, its company image, objectives and predominant management style.

The mentor advises the mentee on self-presentation and behaviour so that he or she can fit into the company's formal culture. Mentees learn how to promote themselves within the organisation, when to be noticed as an individual, and when to be seen working collaboratively. In one large multinational, the primary aim of the mentoring scheme was to help 'invisible' people in the finance department manage their reputation within the organisation in general.

A mentee learns how to operate successfully within the informal culture. The mentor helps the mentee work through the internal company politics by identifying the key decision-makers in the company and the executives who have the real power. As one senior executive comments:

> If you do not know the rules of the game, you cannot operate. The only way to know these rules is to be invited by an insider to participate.

Career advice and advancement

A mentor can act as a role model – a tangible symbol of what the mentee can achieve in the future. As a role model, the mentor helps the mentee to focus career aspirations and turn them into realistic objectives. This is a double-edged sword, of course. The mentee has to beware that he or she does not adopt the mentor's weaknesses as well as his or her strengths!

The mentee learns how to move up the promotion ladder. When the mentor is more senior and more experienced in corporate politics, he or she can help the mentee choose which jobs or projects to take and when to take them.

A female mentee in the social services was advised by her mentor to apply for a position she felt was unattainable. She comments:

> Before the internal interviews my mentor kept dropping my name to other senior administrative officers. He also frequently mentioned me to his own superior. Two other people in the department also applied for the vacancy. There was a woman on my level who had four years' experience and a man a grade higher. Everyone was very surprised when I got the promotion, since it was virtually unknown for someone of my age and experience to jump three levels.

Sometimes the mentor may suggest a total reorientation of career direction and may recommend a decrease or increase in the pace of advancement. One young manager recalls his attitude before he had a mentor:

> I was never sure about the timing of my career – when I should try to move upward or when I should stay in one position. I thought I ought to understand a job completely before I applied for promotion. Then a senior executive took an interest in my career and told me that if I stayed too long in one job I would probably get stuck there since I would not be recognised as a high-flyer. He advised me to apply for a post two grades above my current one. I didn't think I'd get it – but I did.

In traditional US mentoring, the mentor acts as a kind of sponsor, increasing the visibility of the mentee at executive levels by frequently describing how well his or her charge is progressing. The mentor may involve the mentee in his or her own projects and bring the mentee into executive meetings, inviting him or her to speak up. The mentor will brief the mentee beforehand on how to behave, and give background on other subjects scheduled to be discussed.

Within the context of developmental mentoring, the mentee gains a sounding-board who will also help him or her think through the decision-making process, through which the mentee selects between career options. The mentor helps the mentee identify what he or she values, and helps assess each option against his or her personal values and goals. As a result, the mentee gradually becomes more self-confident in making career choices and more adept at turning down those that are likely to lead to blind alleys.

Managerial tutorage

A mentee may gain an insight into management processes through observing his or her mentor closely. The mentor provides an example of effective management and successful leadership and so accelerates the mentee's learning pace. This will apply only where the mentor and mentee are close enough in location/function for the mentee to observe in the normal course of work – or when the mentor specifically invites the mentee to shadow him or her (for example, in making a presentation.) An American mentee at Unisys comments:

> *A mentor teaches the invaluable lesson of people management to a mentee who is often straight out of management school. He may know all about cost-benefit analysis and be an economic wizard – but he needs to be shown, for example, the importance of building support teams. A mentor has the experience to teach this.*

A mentor is able to use his or her knowledge of the organisation to facilitate the mentee's access to areas otherwise closed. As a result, the mentee better understands how the organisation functions. Interviews with 'graduated' mentees reveal that one of the most valuable parts of the relationship is frequent discussion of how the business works and why middle and senior management do not do things the way the mentee would.

My own experience of being guided in this way remains fresh in my mind, although it happened some 25 years ago. As a young junior manager in the publishers McGraw-Hill, I was convinced my boss's boss, the publisher, had no idea what he was doing. So many decisions he made appeared to be irrational. Then he retired and his successor took me under his wing. Although there was a reporting line through my boss, we developed a strong rapport, especially as we travelled together on sales calls to major advertisers. John spent much of the time asking me about my job, but also talked to me about his own role and the context of the decisions he had to make. After a while, I realised that his predecessor was not as stupid as I had thought – he had simply been operating at a level of management more complex than I had previously been exposed to. As I understood this more deeply, I applied what I was learning to my own department, and soon found myself promoted. I had, in effect, graduated to a new level of thinking that opened new doors for me.

A mentee has a legitimate source of advice and information in the mentor. For example, Jenny Blake found:

It was very difficult to sell to the Middle East, especially since I was a woman and not allowed to go there. My mentor was in charge of the Middle East marketing section and was able to give me invaluable advice. He made me aware of important cultural differences and expectations when I was dealing with foreign marketing representatives – for instance, how they expected to be treated with respect and to be made a fuss of.

A junior manager describes the problem he faced without such a figure:

Often a young manager has to try to gather information without betraying his ignorance. It is a very risky business. To get ahead you have to supply the right answers and not ask the wrong questions.

In a mentoring relationship the mentee can ask naïve questions in an unthreatening atmosphere. Helen Martin, a mentor at BP Chemicals, feels that

a mentor is not an agony aunt or a miracle cure for all problems. We are simply people who have probably experienced similar situations in the past. We can therefore help individuals to find the best way to tackle an issue themselves.

Leadership development

Besides teaching managerial and people management skills, mentoring between senior and junior people reveals to the mentee how power is gained and wielded within the company. This is frequently a crucial lesson and is one of the most powerful sources of motivation for a young manager. A business school education may teach valuable theoretical skills but it cannot normally teach a manager how to exercise and feel comfortable with power, nor can it give him or her the confidence to make a major deal on his or her own initiative, take calculated risks or launch a new product. The mentor becomes a valuable sounding-board for difficult decisions and for developing the skills of judgement.

A conscience and guide

One of the behavioural aspects that has impressed me about many of my mentees, particularly those at senior levels in organisations, is how easily I become a kind of conscience for them. Often a week or so before our next meeting they will recall all the actions they said they were going to take. Not wanting to admit that they have not dealt with them, they tend to switch focus from more day-to-day issues so they can report progress to me. It is not that I have any authority over them, or seek to give approval or disapproval – what drives them is their own self-image and self-esteem.

Even when the mentor is not there, some mentees find they can use the mentoring process to address issues that they need to deal with. A quote from one of my mentees:

I do try to have conversations with you in my thoughts, to see if I can imagine what you'd say to me if told you some of this stuff. Occasionally it sort of works, because I start to see things from the point of view I envisage you might take, and think about the kinds of questions you might ask me, to make me consider other perspectives (like: Who am I trying to prove things to and why?). Needless to say, when I do actually write to you, your reply always contains the unexpected and unpredictable.

POTENTIAL DOWNSIDES FOR THE MENTEE

Having a mentor is not always a blessing. Mentors who want to relive their own careers through their mentee, who 'want to stop you making the mistakes I did' or who have their own agenda for the mentee, can be stifling. Indeed, there is some evidence that having an overbearing mentor is a relatively common cause for young graduates to change employer. Conflict between mentor and line manager in another context can sometimes spill over into the mentee's relationship with either or both. Conversely, having a line manager and mentor who are too cosy can also leave the mentee feeling exposed and reluctant to be too open in mentoring discussions.

Although it is rare in developmental mentoring, in sponsoring mentoring it is common for the relationship to develop unhealthy levels of dependence and for mentor and mentee to end up competing with each other for positions.

Finally, mentors who are locked into advice-giving mode may sometimes give the wrong advice. Mentees need to have the personal strength and awareness to make their own minds up about what they should do, even if the mentor is unhappy about it.

In general, the downsides of mentoring for the mentee emerge only when the mentors are poor or the programme is poorly designed and/or implemented.

THE CASE TO THE MENTOR

All the surveys and reviews I have conducted in recent years to evaluate the outcomes of mentoring programmes have indicated that the most frequent and most powerful benefits for mentors are:

- the learning they take from the experience, both in having to explain intuitive reasoning and in listening to a different perspective (ie the problems mentees have with their bosses often cause mentors to reflect on similar issues their direct reports may have with them!)

- the opportunity to make a reflective space in a hectic daily schedule

- the satisfaction of knowing that they have made a difference to someone else

- the intellectual challenge of working on issues for which they do not have to take personal responsibility and that may take them into unfamiliar territory

- increased skills base and reputation.

Mentors questioned in the Industrial Society survey (1995) list the main benefits as prompting reassessment of their own views and leadership style, awareness of the views of more junior staff, a broader perspective, and discovering talent. Other benefits recorded were 'useful roles for plateaued managers' and that mentoring was good for their own career progression. Field experience suggests that when mentees are unaware of how much their mentors are getting out of the relationship, they are constrained in how much use they make of it.

Learning by the mentor

Mentors learn from mentees in a variety of ways.

Firstly, it often occurs that the problems the mentee describes with his or her own manager sound horribly like the mirror image of issues the mentor has with one of his or her direct reports, prompting the mentor to reflect on his or her own behaviour.

Secondly, explaining concepts to someone else is a good way to reinforce good practice in oneself. (Being seen as a role model also puts some pressure on the mentor to live up to his or her own values.)

Thirdly, the mentee is a superb resource of different experience, from which the mentor can extract learning. So much so that some companies now encourage mentoring pairs to be as different as they can tolerate. A good example is the following, recounted to me by the head of diversity in a public sector organisation:

> *We had a senior manager who simply wouldn't take the diversity message on board. He wasn't hostile, but he was dismissive – it simply wasn't enough of an issue to warrant his time or that of his direct reports. I took the gamble of asking him to become the mentor of a younger black man, who had potential to go far in the organisation. Shortly after that, he was promoted to become a regional manager. I met him on a train about six months into the mentoring relationship. He sat down beside me and said: 'My region is a hotbed of racism. What can I do about it?' The transformation had been achieved through listening to his mentee and seeing the world for the first time through black eyes.*

The process of climbing the corporate ladder often means missing out on new ideas, techniques and technologies. There never seems to be the time for catching up, and at a certain stage it becomes embarrassing to admit ignorance. Directing the learning experiences of the mentee gives the mentor the excuse he or she needs to devote the time to developing his or her own knowledge too. It is also often acknowledged that the best way to learn is to teach. Some companies see mentees as a source of practical help for the mentor, while Midland Bank (now HSBC) has found that

> *Mentors have identified a need to increase their own business awareness of Midland Group in order to be better placed to respond to mentees.*

Opportunities to reflect

The more senior people become in an organisation, the less thinking time they seem to have. Many mentors regard their mentoring sessions as a welcome opportunity to adopt a change of pace. Some also report that the discipline of doing so helps them take reflective space to consider their own issues, too.

Intellectual challenge

The most successful mentoring relationships almost always involve a heightened level of mutual challenge, based upon the quality of trust and respect between the two partners. Says one mentor:

I wouldn't say I'm coasting in my job, but there's not a lot of intellectual stretch in it for me. But the problems my mentee brings me don't have straightforward answers. It's clear he relishes the discussions, and lately we've branched out into wider areas of company policy. As a result I've taken some ideas for change to my director, and there's a high chance my job will expand to take some of them forward.

Personal satisfaction

Helping a promising younger employee make progress can be a challenging and stimulating experience for a mentor, especially if his or her own career has reached a temporary or permanent plateau. Some managers whose careers have reached a real or perceived plateau find the challenge of mentoring both rewarding and stimulating and have been motivated to put new effort into their own career planning.

Mentors often find the mentoring relationship rewarding in many other ways – for example, in pride when the mentee achieves personal goals. Mentors also gain a sense of purpose in seeing the values and culture of an organisation handed to a new generation and in thinking more carefully about company policies. Says an industrial company with a long-running mentoring programme:

Mentoring has made us question traditional thinking and practices, firstly to clarify them in our own minds before explaining them to our mentees, but also in not just defending them when challenged through the innocent, unadulterated eyes of the newcomer who has not yet been influenced by our culture.

Increased skills base and reputation

A mentor who identifies promising employees acquires a reputation for having a keen insight into the needs of the company. This enhances his or her status with peers. The international accounting firm Merrill Lynch & Co. constructed a formal system of rewarding its mentors. Mentors' names are included in regularly circulated reports about mentees' accomplishments. Mentors are personally thanked by top management and are invited to be presenters at mentor briefing sessions which are run for new participants. A spokesman for the firm explains:

We feel we need to reward our mentors visibly and link their success publicly to the success of the mentoring programme.

One thing the mentor does not receive, and should not be led to expect from the scheme, is a direct payment or bonus to compensate him or her for the time and effort spent. An argument against such payments is that developing others is an integral part of every manager's job. A more powerful argument is that mentorship has to be built on friendship and is a close and personal relationship. So turning it into a paid service is likely to hinder the relaxed and informal atmosphere necessary between mentor and mentee. In theory, this can become a problem if the company links human development objectives to a bonus scheme as part of the annual performance appraisal. In practice, the trick is to ensure that the mentor is neither especially rewarded nor penalised for this part of his or her job.

A few companies reward their mentors with status, inviting them to attend annual or biannual lunches or dinners with top management, where people strategies are discussed in open forum. Access to top management thinking – the inside track – is a prized commodity in most organisations.

Mentors at Pilkington Glass, proponents of one of the earliest graduate mentoring schemes in Europe, perceived the following benefits:

- We clarify and question our perception of the company.
- We see the company through fresh eyes.
- We improve our abilities so we have more to offer the mentee.
- We see people work in different ways depending on whether they are theorists, activists, etc.
- It offers a new challenge.
- It offers a new learning experience.
- We understand the trauma new recruits experience and can be more sympathetic to others undergoing change.

DOWNSIDES FOR THE MENTOR

As with the mentee, there are few significant downsides for mentors in carrying out the role, if they do it well, other than that this is yet another demand on their time. For this reason I generally advise new mentors to think very carefully before committing to more than one or two relationships, or they may not do them justice. Some of the other downsides I have observed over the years include:

- the breaking of confidentiality by the mentee (largely the mentor's fault)
- resentment on the part of direct reports that they are not receiving similar time and effort invested in their development to that the mentor spends with the mentee
- loss of face when a succession of mentoring relationships fail (usually a sign of poor mentoring, but occasionally the result of a run of circumstances)
- having an overdemanding mentee (my favourite is the young graduate who came to see his mentor several times a day for reassurance – it took a threat by the mentor to throw the graduate through the window to stop this behaviour – by which time the relationship had nowhere to go!).

THE CASE TO THE LINE MANAGER

It is surprising how little attention is paid to the line manager as a stakeholder in the mentoring relationship, yet he or she can make or break it. All too often line managers only see the downsides of having a direct report mentored – the mentee will be taking more time away from his or her work for mentoring meetings, and *what are they saying about me?* The latter is a very valid concern. As a good working estimate, at least 90 per cent of mentoring pairs spend some time discussing the mentee's relationship with his or her boss. This seems to hold broadly true at all levels, from new recruit at the lowest levels to chief executive.

Where the line manager sees the positives, however, it benefits everyone. When the mentee can discuss relationships with his or her boss and other working colleagues within the mentoring meeting, it allows the mentee to put his or her own and other people's behaviour and expectations into perspective. The mentee develops, with the mentor's help, better strategies for tackling issues around these relationships. If the mentee has a difficult conversation to initiate, he or she can practise it first with the mentor. As a result, relationships between the line manager and the mentee, and between the mentee and other colleagues, can be substantially improved.

The line manager also has access to a second opinion. If he or she feels the mentee is not understanding or committing to something important, the line manager can recommend the mentee to take it up with his or her mentor. It sometimes happens that the line manager sees this as a great opportunity to dump all that troublesome development stuff on someone else. This is a wasted opportunity that could be used for investing more time in the coaching role and raising the performance of the whole team.

SUMMARY

Listing the benefits of mentoring is useful in developing the general argument in favour of the process. There is a deeper reason, however, for developing a clarity about the expected outcomes of any mentoring programme. Where people have high clarity about the organisation's expectations from a mentoring programme, they are more likely to be clear about the objectives of their own relationship, and this, in turn, appears to lead to more productive pairings. As we shall examine in subsequent chapters, knowing what you want out of mentoring is critical to getting what you want!

5

What makes an effective mentor, an effective mentee?

It may seem an obvious point that mentors and mentees should be selected (or encouraged to come forward) within the context of the programme objectives. The qualities that are relevant for mentors and mentees in a programme aimed to help at-risk teenagers are not the same as those for people engaged in a mentoring programme aimed at people undertaking their first general manager job overseas. Yes, there will be generic similarities – for example, the mentees' need to understand and come to terms with their respective environments, and the mentors' need to be able to empathise with the situations the mentee describes – but the circumstances and the purpose of the relationship defines the need in terms of expected behaviours and competencies.

Mentoring is a disciplined process, although it has few rules. The organisation should decide and explain carefully who it wants to mentor and why, the criteria for selection, and who will do the selecting. The criteria will vary from company to company but should always be drawn against the background of this question: 'How much will this person gain from a mentoring relationship?'

In this chapter we explore some of the generics and set out some principles for managing selection and matching processes.

CHOOSING MENTORS

In theory, at least, the mentee should be the starting point for selecting the mentor. In practice, some organisations have begun by creating a pool of mentors and gone looking for suitable mentees for them (or sent them off to find their own!). This has the disadvantage of creating some level of obligation to find a mentee for any would-be mentor, no matter how incompetent he or she may be in the role, and risks making the whole process mentor-driven.

Every manager's job should entail a significant amount of developing other people, and indeed some companies make it a virtual condition of each manager's advancement. In practice, however, some people are better cut out for it than others. Moreover, the ability to act as a mentor will often vary according to the manager's own stage of career development. For example, someone seeking or undergoing a major change in his or her own career development may not have the mental energy to spare for someone else's issues.

In selecting the mentor, a company must have a clear sense of the qualities that make a good developer of other people's potential. These qualities may differ from company to company, even from division to division. Equally, the ideal mentor for one person may be a disaster for another. It follows, naturally, that companies will disagree on the criteria they use to identify good mentors. Gerald O'Callaghan, formerly responsible for BP Chemicals' mentoring scheme, states:

> Mentors are not picked for any superhuman qualities – though some may fall into that category. Most are experienced, well-balanced professionals and managers who are interested in developing young people and broadening their own contribution to the company. They are among the best staff we have.

There have been numerous attempts to define the competencies of a mentor, most of them flawed by a failure to define to begin with what role is being measured. There is also a great deal of confusion in the literature between practical skills or competencies (what mentors do/how they do it) and functions/outcomes (the results of the mentoring relationship). My own view of the skill set has evolved significantly over the years and is now most succinctly summarised in Figure 7.

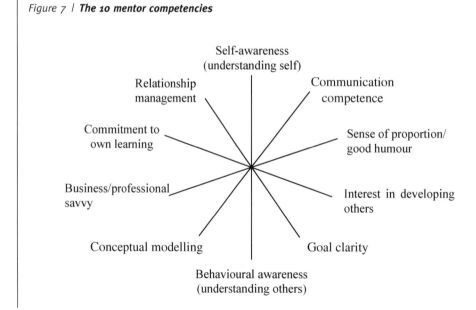

Figure 7 | *The 10 mentor competencies*

[The following section on the 10 mentor competencies is taken from Clutterbuck (2000a) and is reproduced with kind permission of the publishers, the Association for Management Education and Development.]

1 Self-awareness (understanding self)

Mentors need high self-awareness in order to recognise and manage their own behaviours within the helping relationship and to use empathy appropriately. The activist, task-focused manager often has relatively little insight into these areas – indeed, he or she may actively avoid reflection on such issues, depicting them as 'soft' and of low priority. Such attitudes and learned behaviours may be difficult to break.

Providing managers with psychometric tests and other forms of insight-developing question-naire can be useful if they are open to insights in those areas. However, it is easy to dismiss such feedback, even when it also comes from external sources, such as working colleagues.

Some managers actively seek psychometric analysis, yet fail to internalise it – to carry out the inner dialogue essential to carrying knowledge through to action. Not that all personality insights should necessarily lead to action; in many cases, the role of internal dialogue may be to help the person accept that a behaviour pattern or perceived weakness can reasonably be lived with.

Interviews with mentors and mentees indicate that having some level of personality and motivational insight is useful for building rapport in the early stages of a relationship. 'This is me/this is you' – is a good starting-point for open behaviours. People who have low self-awareness can be helped in a number of ways. One is through dialogue with a trained counsellor/facilitator, helping them relate psychometric and other behavioural feedback to specific actions and behaviours. By learning how to think through such issues for themselves, they may become more effective at doing the same for others.

Figure 8 shows a useful way of looking at this kind of approach to building self-awareness.

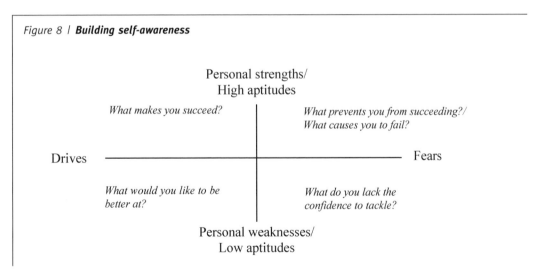

*Figure 8 | **Building self-awareness***

Personal strengths/
High aptitudes

What makes you succeed?

*What prevents you from succeeding?/
What causes you to fail?*

Drives — — Fears

*What would you like to be
better at?*

*What do you lack the
confidence to tackle?*

Personal weaknesses/
Low aptitudes

If nothing else, the model helps open up some of the hidden boxes in the Johari window! An important debate here is whether low self-awareness is the result of low motivation to explore the inner self (disinterest), or high motivation to avoid such exploration, or simply an inability to make complex emotional and rational connections (in which case there may be physiological aspects to consider as well). The approach in helping someone develop self-awareness will be different in each case and is likely to be least effective in bringing about personal change.

2 Behavioural awareness (understanding others)

Like self-awareness, understanding how others behave and why they do so is a classic component of emotional intelligence. To help others manage their relationships, the mentor must have reasonably good insight into patterns of behaviour between individuals and groups of people. Predicting the consequences of specific behaviours or courses of action is one of the many practical applications of this insight.

Developing clearer insight into the behaviours of others comes from frequent observation and reflection. Supervision groups can help the mentor recognise common patterns of behaviour by creating opportunities for rigorous analysis.

3 Business or professional savvy

There is not a great deal to be done here in the short term – there are very few shortcuts to experience and judgement. However, the facilitator can help the potential mentor understand the need for developing judgement and plan how to acquire relevant experience.

Again, the art of purposeful reflection is a valuable support in building this competence. By reviewing the learning from a variety of experiences, the manager widens his or her range of templates and develops a sense of patterns in events. The more frequently he or she is able to combine stretching experience with focused reflection – either internally or in a dialogue with others – the more substantial and rapid the acquisition of judgement.

A useful method of helping people develop business savvy is to create learning sets, where a skilled facilitator encourages people to share their experience and look for patterns.

4 Sense of proportion/good humour

Is good humour a competence? I would argue strongly that it is. Laughter, used appropriately, is invaluable in developing rapport, in helping people to see matters from a different perspective, in releasing emotional tension. It is also important that mentor and mentee should enjoy the sessions they have together. Enthusiasm is far more closely associated with learning than boredom is!

Can adults develop a good sense of humour if they do not already have one? Probably not easily. However, a good deal of pessimistic attitude and cynicism derive from a feeling of disempowerment and a perceived lack of control over one's circumstances. Such attitude changes can be created by helping people become more at ease with themselves, with their role in the organisation and their potential to influence their environment. The most obvious way to make that happen – apart from wholesale culture change within the organisation – is for the individual to have his or her own mentor.

In practice, good humour is a vehicle for achieving a sense of proportion – a broader perspective that places the organisation's goals and culture in the wider social and business context. People acquire this kind of perspective by ensuring that they balance their day-to-day involvement with work tasks against a portfolio of other interests. Some of these may be related to work – for example, developing a broader strategic understanding of how the business sector is evolving. Others are unrelated to work and may encompass science, philosophy or any other intellectually stimulating endeavour. In general, the broader the scope of knowledge and experience the mentor can apply, the better sense of proportion he or she can bring.

5 Communication competence

Communication is not a single skill: it is a combination of a number of skills. Those most important for the mentor include:

- listening – opening the mind to what the other person is saying, demonstrating interest/attention, encouraging him or her to speak, holding back on filling the silences

- observing as receiver – being open to the visual and other non-verbal signals, recognising what is not said

- parallel processing – analysing what the other person is saying, reflecting on it, preparing responses; effective communicators do all of these in parallel, slowing down the dialogue as needed to ensure that they do not overemphasise preparing responses at the expense of analysis and reflection; equally, they avoid becoming so mired in their internal thoughts that they respond inadequately or too slowly

- projecting – crafting words and their emotional 'wrapping' in a manner appropriate for the situation and the recipient(s)

- observing as projector – being open to the visual and other non-verbal signals, as clues to what the recipient is hearing/understanding; adapting tone, volume, pace and language appropriately

- exiting – concluding a dialogue or segment of dialogue with clarity and alignment of understanding (ensuring that the message has been received in both directions).

Some tools to help develop these competencies are *neurolinguistic programming* (if used with a sense of proportion) and *situational communication*.

Situational communication, developed by the *item* Group with help from Birkbeck College, helps people understand the communication requirements of different commonplace situations and focus on the development of specific skills in those situations. It thus has a very high utility factor. Alongside situational communication is a very practical method of diagnosing communication styles, which enables the individual to become more self-aware of his or her own style preferences and to recognise the preferences of others. Good mentors will generally need a strong sense of situation and a high degree of adaptability between styles.

6 Conceptual modelling

Effective mentors have a portfolio of models they can draw upon to help mentees understand the issues they face. These models can be self-generated (eg the result of personal experience), drawn from elsewhere (eg models of company structure, interpersonal behaviours, strategic planning, career planning) or – at the highest level of competence – generated on the spot as an immediate response.

According to the situation and the learning styles of the mentee, it may be appropriate to present these models in verbal or visual form. Or the mentor may not present them at all – simply use them as the framework for asking penetrating questions.

Developing the skills of conceptual modelling takes time, once again. It requires a lot of reading, often beyond the normal range of materials that cross the individual's desk. Training in presentation skills and how to design simple diagrams can also help. But the most effective way can be for the mentor to seize every opportunity to explain complex ideas in a variety of ways, experimenting to see what works with different audiences. Eventually, there develops an intuitive, instinctive understanding of how best to put across a new idea.

7 Commitment to one's own continued learning

Effective mentors become role models for self-managed learning. They seize opportunities to experiment and take part in new experiences. They read widely and are reasonably efficient at setting and following personal development plans. They actively seek and use behavioural feedback from others.

These skills can be developed with practice. Again, having a role model to follow for themselves is a good starting-point.

8 Strong interest in developing others

Effective mentors have an innate interest in achieving through others and in helping others recognise and achieve their potential. This instinctive response is important in establishing and maintaining rapport and in enthusing the mentee, building confidence in what he or she could become.

While it is possible to 'switch on' someone to the self-advantage of helping others, it is probably not feasible to stimulate an altruistic response.

9 Building and maintaining rapport/relationship management

The skills of rapport-building are difficult to define. When asked to describe rapport in their experience, managers' observations can be distilled into five characteristics:

- trust – Will they do what they say? Will they keep confidences?

- focus – Are they concentrating on me? Are they listening without judging?

- empathy – Do they have goodwill towards me? Do they try to understand my feelings, and viewpoints?

- congruence – Do they acknowledge and accept my goals?
- empowerment – Is their help aimed at helping me stand on my own feet as soon as is practical?

To a considerable extent, the skills of building and maintaining rapport are contained in the other competencies already described. However, additional help in developing rapport-building skills may be provided through situational analysis – creating opportunities for the individual to explore with other people how and why he or she feels comfortable and uncomfortable with them in various circumstances. This kind of self-knowledge can be invaluable in developing more sensitive responses to other people's needs and emotions.

The mentor can also be encouraged to think about the contextual factors in creating rapport. Avoiding meeting on the mentor's home ground (eg in his or her office) may be an obvious matter, but where would the mentee feel most comfortable? Sensitivity to how the meeting environment affects the mentoring dialogue can be developed simply by talking the issues through, both in formal or informal training and with the mentee.

10 Goal clarity

The mentor must be able to help the mentee sort out what he or she wants to achieve and why. This is quite hard to do if you do not have the skills to set and pursue clear goals of your own.

Goal clarity appears to derive from a mixture of skills including systematic analysis and decisiveness. Like so many of the other mentoring competencies, it may best be developed through opportunities to reflect and to practise.

WHAT MENTORS DO

In the first edition of this book I incorporated a useful acronym from a North American article, which maintained that the mentor:

- **M**anages the relationship
- **E**ncourages
- **N**urtures
- **T**eaches
- **O**ffers mutual respect
- **R**esponds to the mentee's needs.

Once again, views have moved on. Although the notion of the mentor managing the relationship still holds favour in some US companies, the wider global expectation is for the mentor to assist the mentee in taking over the management of the relationship. Similarly, when it comes to responding to the mentee's needs, it is no longer seen as a good idea for the mentor to be more than minimally interventionist. Rather, the mentor helps the mentee work out his or her own solutions. The concepts of encouragement, nurturing, teaching and offering mutual respect remain largely unchanged, however, and we repeat those notes here (with minor amendments) for background information.

THE MENTOR WHO ENCOURAGES AND MOTIVATES

The ability to encourage and motivate is another important interpersonal skill that the mentor must have in abundance if the relationship with the mentee is to reach its full potential.

The mentor must be able to recognise the ability of the mentee and make it clear to the mentee that he or she believes in the mentee's capacity to progress within the company. The mentor must be willing to let the mentee turn to him or her for as long as needed, as well as be willing to help the mentee eventually become independent.

The mentor encourages the mentee through recognising the different roles he or she can play. For a certain period the mentor can be a reassuring parental figure to whom the mentee can turn for support and sympathy. The mentor must also at this stage be willing to let the mentee identify with him or her and use him or her as a role model. At other stages of the relationship, the mentor can encourage the mentee to become more independent and make individual decisions.

One mentor in a Civil Service department recalls how difficult it was to learn this lesson:

I had this intelligent individual who was highly motivated. I expected his progress to be extremely rapid, but was surprised to find that he seemed to depend on me for quite some time. I was worried about it and considered whether I ought to try to force him somehow to make his own decisions unaided by me. Eventually I decided to go at his pace and not the pace I expected. He is now at a higher level than me in the company, but recently came to me to thank me for not rushing him in that first year. He explained he had found it very difficult to adjust to his new job and had found the new pressure especially hard to cope with. Apparently, my support and encouragement had kept him going through it all.

The ability to encourage and motivate is an especially important skill for the mentor if, as we discussed in Chapter 4, the company has a deliberate policy of not promoting high-flyers until they have a broad base of experience. If these people are to be prevented from seeking faster promotion elsewhere, the mentor has to help them extract a high degree of job satisfaction from their experiences now and let them know they will reap the rewards for their patience later in their career.

One corporate mentor explains:

We get so many MBAs coming straight from college who expect to race up the promotion ladder. Without a mentor to explain the system to them, few of them realise that this is just not the way we operate. If we discover a talented individual, we allocate them to different areas of the company before we promote them so that they understand and have been directly involved in all aspects of the business.

A young manager in a small British defence firm emphasises the point with reference to the difference the support of a senior manager made to his career:

I graduated with an engineering degree and immediately took my MBA. I then successfully applied for the position of technical manager, which had just been newly created, in a defence firm. I found my new job extremely difficult because I was dealing with engineers who were obviously far more experienced than I and whose technical knowledge far outmatched mine. They plainly resented my presence. A few were even openly hostile to me. Fortunately, since my position was new to the company itself, a senior manager had been asked to help me as much as possible. He supported and encouraged me. Sometimes it was only this which stopped me from leaving. More importantly, he helped me to recognise that my difficulties were not caused by my own incompetence or failure, as I had originally thought, but that in fact the engineers' hostility had another cause and was aimed at my position rather than at me personally. He explained that the company had been trying to get the structure of the technical side of the company more into line with central management. I was just unlucky to be caught in the middle of a war between management and the engineers.

Armed with the knowledge that he was fully supported by top management, this young manager was able to ride the storm until he won the respect of the engineering staff.

THE MENTOR WHO NURTURES

The mentor must be able to create an open, candid atmosphere that will encourage the mentee to confide in and trust him or her. The mentor is there to draw out the mentee and help discover his or her identity within the organisation. With the help of the mentor, the mentee undertakes self-assessment and discovers where his or her skills, aspirations and interests lie. Most importantly, the mentor must be able to listen to the mentee and ask open-ended questions that will draw out the less experienced person.

One key test of the mentor who nurtures is a track record of bringing along subordinates. If his or her department has provided a consistent breeding-ground for talented young supervisors and managers, then the chances are high that he or she will make a good mentor for people from other departments.

THE MENTOR WHO TEACHES

This is a skill that the mentor may need to be taught, because being a really good teacher does not come naturally to many people. Highly ambitious, self-motivated people (and the description applies to most people who make it to top management) often lack the patience to teach. Yet the mentor must know how to help the mentee maximise his or her opportunities to learn. The mentor does this by creating a stimulating environment that consistently challenges the mentee to apply theory to the real world of management.

A mentor may teach his or her mentee using the following methods:

- The mentor holds 'what if?' sessions in which he or she guides the mentee in problem-solving discussions to encourage him or her to discover as many alternatives as possible.

- The mentor discusses with the mentee real problems the mentor is currently dealing with or has recently dealt with. Rather than expand upon the cleverness of his or her own solutions, the mentor asks the mentee what course of action he or she would take. The mentor can often complete the analysis by telling the mentee the solutions he or she actually devised and why they were chosen. In this way, through mini internal case studies, the mentor gives the mentee an insight into decision-making in higher-level jobs.

- The mentor plays devil's advocate. In a protective environment, the mentor teaches the mentee how to assert his or her opinions and influence the listener in difficult situations. The mentor plays aggressive and threatening roles so that the mentee learns to handle stressful and potentially explosive situations.

A vice-chairman in an advertising company was helped in his career by a senior executive in the corporation. This mentor invited opposition from his mentee and frequently acted in a domineering and brusque manner. The mentor's aim was to help develop in his mentee an aggressiveness that he considered was essential for success in that field. The vice-chairman comments:

Before I met my mentor I was not particularly forceful. However, when I talked to him I found I had the choice either to be chewed up or to assert myself. He constantly pushed me in these one-to-one confrontations so that now when I talk to a client I have developed a way of expressing my opinions with weight and force.

THE MENTOR WHO OFFERS MUTUAL RESPECT

An essential ingredient in any mentoring relationship is mutual respect between the two partners. If the mentee does not respect and trust his or her mentor's opinions, advice and influence – and vice versa – the benefits from the relationship will be severely limited. Programme co-ordinators must remember that a mentee's attitude towards the mentor is inevitably influenced by the mentor's general reputation within the company.

To be more precise, the mentee will:

- assess the mentor's professional reputation by scrutinising his or her past performance; if a mentor has been involved with too many failed projects, the mentee is likely to feel that a close alliance with that person will do his or her career little good

- assess the mentor's interpersonal skills – for example, a mentee may feel that a rewarding relationship could not be established with a mentor who is heard of only through memos and telephone calls

- assess the mentor's status with his or her colleagues; if the mentor commands respect and esteem from peers, the mentee feels that his or her career will benefit from being associated with the mentor

- assess the mentor's corporate alliances; the mentee must believe that his or her mentor has enough influence in the organisation to make a tangible difference to his or her career.

This latter point illustrates yet again the evolution that has taken place in our thinking about mentoring since these words were first penned. The emphasis on career outcomes expressed here has now generally been balanced by an equal or greater emphasis on the personal development outcomes, which may or may not have a direct impact on career achievement. Respect within developmental mentoring comes less from an appreciation of what the mentor can do for the mentee than from what he or she can help the mentee do on his or her own.

Checklist – ideal characteristics to seek in a mentor

- Look for someone who:

- already has a good record for developing other people

- has a genuine interest in seeing younger people advance and can relate to their problems

- has a wide range of current skills to pass on

- has a good understanding of the organisation, how it works and where it is going

- combines patience with good interpersonal skills and an ability to work in an unstructured programme

- has sufficient time to devote to the relationship

- can command a mentee's respect

- has his or her own network of contacts and influence

- is still keen to learn.

THE MENTOR FROM HELL

The mentor from hell exists – at least in the minds of mentees who have been unfortunate enough to encounter him or her. Consider this story from a young manager, recalling his days as a graduate mentee:

> *Once every six months I'd be summoned to the great man's presence. I'd come slightly early and he would always be running late. I'd sit in the ante-room, where his secretary made sure I didn't steal any paperclips. As I was shown in, he'd always be putting away my file – reminding himself of who I was. Then he'd talk at me solidly for over an hour. Finally, he'd ask if I'd found it useful. I never had the courage to tell him the truth ... !*

This mentor hadn't a clue and probably didn't want to know how to do the job properly anyway – it might have spoiled the ego trip. He might have been horrified to be told that good mentors speak for less than 20 per cent of the time, address issues raised by the mentee, and expect to engage in quality dialogue on a much more frequent basis than once every six months.

Some other common toxic mentors include:

- people who rush around 'helping' others in order to avoid addressing their own issues and often end up transferring their problem into the mentee's situation
- people who have an alternative agenda
- people who take umbrage when the mentee adopts a different solution from the one they have proposed
- people who are not switched on to their own learning.

CHOOSING MENTEES

'So what's the business problem?' That's the first question I typically ask when working with an organisation to design a mentoring programme, because without a clear target group with a specific issue to manage, it will be very difficult to establish whether the project has been worthwhile. Very often there is a mixture of objectives, but the most common seem to be:

- to retain key staff
- to overcome institutional barriers to progress for disadvantaged groups
- to build bridges between parts of the organisation
- to support culture change, especially after a merger or major acquisition
- to support a competency programme.

Defining the business (or community) issue largely defines the selection criteria for mentees, whether these are used to identify people through some central co-ordinating mechanism or to enable people to decide for themselves whether to apply. In the Cabinet Office's Disability Leadership Programme, for example, potential mentees nominate themselves but receive endorsement from their department and have to attend an interview process that selects those who will take part in the full scheme, complete with bursary, and those who will simply receive a mentor.

At high-tech company Araya (formerly Lucent) mentees nominate themselves on to a broad self-development programme whose members meet monthly to learn together. Although intended originally for high- and low-performers, the programme has attracted a wide range of people, each of whom is offered a choice of two mentors.

Mentoring schemes for high-flyers tend to have some element of evaluation built in to ensure that they have the commitment and potential to make effective use of the opportunity they have been given.

At NatWest Bank the mentoring programme encourages potential high-flyers to move on to the fast track at an early stage. Interested candidates undergo a series of rigorous tests and interviews. If they are deemed to have potential, they then attend a week-long training course where their potential is discussed and they are given practical suggestions for personal development.

Ground rules, which have been learned the hard way in a wide variety of organisations (but that does not stop other companies repeating the mistakes), include:

- Do not assume that everyone in the target group wants to have a mentor. A large financial services company in the City dutifully followed orders from New York and set up mentoring pairs for all its middle-level women, matching them either with more senior women or male executives. In interviews, many of the women reported that they were bemused by the project. While they had had very pleasant lunches, neither they nor the mentors were clear about what the purpose of meeting was, and many felt patronised by what they saw as a heavy-handed approach. Others saw the initiative as some kind of mark of inferiority – 'Somebody has decided I have a problem, but they haven't the balls to tell me what it is,' said one woman.

- Do not assume that any target group sees itself as a group. One company, concerned that hardly anyone had signed up for a mentoring programme for people from ethnic minorities, discovered that the intended beneficiaries saw themselves either in their professional status or from much smaller communities – Muslims and Hindus saw their issues as very different and resented being lumped together.

- Accept that some people may have less need of a mentor at some points in their career than others. Giving the individual some say in when he or she becomes involved increases personal commitment to the process. (A recent example I encountered involved a small group of middle managers who had not met their assigned mentors more than once or twice over almost a year. When quizzed about their reluctance, they explained that the mentor was fine, but not currently needed. Each of them had an excellent and productive developmental relationship with their line manager and with the tutor on the leadership course they were taking. 'Right now, I'm concentrating on applying what I'm learning to my current job and my performance in a couple of skills areas,' explained one. 'I can't cope with any more help at the moment. But I'd expect to make use of my mentor when I need to put all this into the bigger picture and establish some longer-term development goals.')

- Sometimes a mentor is not the most appropriate form of help. Until a few years ago I would routinely recommend companies' setting up mentoring for graduate entrants to provide a mentor from Day 1. Practical experience shows this is usually a mistake. It typically takes three to six months in the organisation before the mentee understands enough of the systems and culture to ask insightful questions, but by this time one or both parties has often become bored and the relationship struggles to get back on course. Organisations are increasingly opting instead for a six-month buddy system in which the graduate is teamed up with a recruit from the previous year who can show him or her the ropes.

THE EFFECTIVE MENTEE

At first sight, it may seem invidious to set out criteria for 'good' mentees. After all, surely the purpose of mentoring is at least partly to help people become more effective. Nonetheless, how the mentee behaves can have a substantial impact on the quality and type of help he or she receives. Moreover, there is a surprisingly wide literature about what mentors are looking for in a mentee. Take the following analysis from the well-respected US author Michael Zey (1984):

- *Intelligence* – the mentee must be able to identify and solve business problems rapidly.

- *Ambition* – the mentee must be gifted and have the ambition to channel his ability into career advancement. The mentor also wants to further his career and looks for a mentee who will advance through the organisation with him.

- *Succession potential* – the mentor also wants a mentee who demonstrates that he is capable of performing the mentor's own job. The mentor wants to be sure that he has groomed a replacement.

- *Strong interpersonal skills* – the mentee must be able to make new alliances for the mentor as well as retaining the ones the mentor has already established.

A study carried out in the USA in 1982, but still not replicated or superseded, adds a further important, if somewhat obvious, characteristic. It found that employees who performed visible, risky and important tasks were three times as likely to form mentoring relationships of their own accord as those who took few risks. It suggests that mentor relationships succeed and are more mutually rewarding if the mentee is chosen for his or her general, all-round reputation for hard work, enthusiasm and ability.

This is the language of sponsorship mentoring rather than developmental mentoring. It assumes that mentoring targets only the elite of the business and should not be wasted on less capable people. Certainly, this is a view that has been increasingly challenged as companies perceive mentoring as a tool of far wider use that can be directed at people of a wide range of abilities and ambitions.

Yet there is some validity in the concept of the 'good' mentee. Successful mentoring relationships (success is defined as occurring when one or both parties achieve significant learning and/or support) are characterised, among other things, by mentees who are:

- realistically ambitious for the relationship, having clear expectations of what it can do for them

- unambiguous about their own role in selecting and bringing issues for discussion

- prepared to take the prime responsibility for meeting arrangements and the agenda

- willing to challenge and be challenged

- able to approach the relationship with respect, good humour and openness

- aware of the obligations the relationship places on them, with regard to their behaviour towards the mentor and to interested third parties, such as their line manager.

The more closely the mentee meets these characteristics, the more he or she (and the mentor) is likely to get out of the relationship. By contrast, mentoring is often difficult to make work in cultures where a high proportion of people adopt an 'outer-directed' view of the world – ie they have low belief in their own capacity to influence events in their favour. Although mentoring relationships can flourish in such an environment, the mentor needs great patience.

Other studies of mentoring relationships, from Scandinavia, suggest that the most effective are those where the mentee is highly proactive and the mentor relatively reactive.

SUMMARY

No one expects mentors or mentees to be perfect. Indeed, the mentoring relationship is one in which developing skills and positive personal characteristics is both the goal and the core of the process. However, in selecting participants in a mentoring programme, it is important to consider what each is able and willing to learn and to contribute. One of the gratifying aspects of the introductory briefings I have given in many companies about to launch mentoring programmes is that so many people who have come with the intent of becoming a mentor decide instead (or as well) to be a mentee, and vice versa!

6

Matching mentors and mentees

One of the advantages of informal mentoring is that would-be mentees can have as many bites at the cherry as they like until they find a relationship that works for them. In formal, structured programmes that is not so easy. Again, there have evolved some practical ground rules that avoid some of the worst problems:

- Avoid 'shotgun marriages' wherever possible. The least successful matches are typically those where the mentor and mentee feel they have been imposed upon each other. Next least successful are those where pairings are nominated by top management. If you cannot allow people some element of choice, at least make sure that participants understand how the matching process has been made. SmithKline Beecham, before merged to become GlaxoSmithKline, installed match-making software that included a variety of information about the mentee's learning needs, the mentor's experience and some general psychometric data intended to avoid strong clashes of learning styles.

  The greatest level of buy-in from participants seems to come from giving the mentee a selection of three potential mentors, whom he or she can meet if he or she wishes. It is very rare for anyone to ask for more than the original three. Making it clear that mentees will make their selection according to the degree of rapport they feel and the closeness of match with their learning need seems to overcome most of the potential problems of mentors feeling turned down.

- Equally, avoid giving people an unguided choice. Experience suggests that many people will select as a mentor someone whom they know well and get on with. Alternatively, they will seek a high-flyer on whose coat-tails they can hang. Neither is likely to lead to a successful mentoring relationship. Too much familiarity allows little grit in the oyster – the amount of learning potential is relatively low. Seeking a high-flyer starts the relationship off with a set of unhealthy expectations. Moreover, the high-flyer may be too preoccupied with his or her own career to give much time to someone else.

- Avoid too great a hierarchy or experience gap between mentor and mentee. Figure 9 illustrates the point.

Figure 9 | *The hierarchy/experience gap between mentor and mentee*

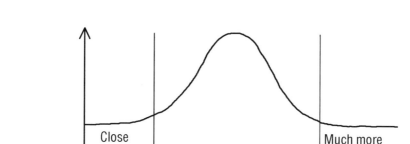

If the experience gap is too narrow, mentor and mentee will have little to talk about. If it is too great, the mentor's experience will be increasingly irrelevant to the mentee. Whereas once upon a time we could broadly say that there should not be more than two layers of hierarchy between mentor and mentee, organisation structures are now so complex and a single layer of management may hide such a wide variation in status, experience and ability that such a simple rule no longer suffices. It is up to the mentee and the programme co-ordinator to establish an appropriate learning distance.

An extension of the same principle is shown in Figure 10.

Figure 10 | *How experience and discipline affect rapport and learning potential*

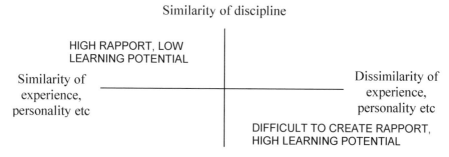

In the top right corner, the relatively immature learner or the person lacking confidence will often feel more comfortable with someone who shares a similar functional background and perhaps common interests and views outside of work. At the other extreme, a highly self-confident, mature learner may welcome the challenge of learning with someone with whom they have very little in common. (A classic case here is the CEO of a local authority whose mentor is a highly educated Indian pharmacist in the same borough. The CEO uses the mentor as a sounding-board on issues that affect the sizeable local ethnic community; the pharmacist has a passionate interest in politics, although only as a passive observer.) Other people may select a mentor who is different enough to give the relationship some learning 'bite' but similar enough to make it easy to build and maintain rapport.

Although this approach seems rather mechanical, it does seem to be how well-informed HR professionals make their instinctive choices about who they should recommend to pair. It also helps in decisions about how close the mentor should be to the mentee in organisation terms. In many modern programmes, the mentor's different perspective is a critical element of the relationship. At a large UK retailer, for example, mentees in the finance division were divided into two groups: those who needed to become more effective in their functional responsibilities, for whom a mentor from finance was provided, and those who were technically proficient but who needed greater commercial awareness, who were given mentors from sales, merchandising and marketing.

- Avoid entanglements between line and off-line relationships.

Most companies with mentoring programmes aimed at managers, for example, prefer to establish the relationship outside the normal working hierarchy. One reason for this is that there are times in the mentoring relationship when both sides need to back off. This is something much easier to do if there is a certain distance between them, either in hierarchical level or departmental function, or both. In addition, the boss-subordinate relationship, with all its entanglements of decisions on pay rises, disciplinary responsibilities and performance appraisal, may work against the openness and candour of the true mentoring relationship. The line manager may also not have a sufficiently wide experience of other job opportunities. Moreover, unless the line manager mentors all his or her direct reports – which would involve a very substantial time commitment – there is likely to be resentment from those people who are not mentored, while those who are become cast as favourites. This does not help build team unity!

- Ensure that mentors are committed to the programme.

A manager who is outstanding in his or her field may at first glance seem to be an ideal candidate for a mentor. It is just this sort of flair and expertise the company needs to pass on. However, if this manager's communication skills are extremely poor, or the manager resents being taken from his or her work because of mentorship obligations, he or she is unlikely to function well in the role. The company, the mentor and the mentee may all suffer in these circumstances.

Such a situation arose in one company where the programme co-ordinators attempted to assign mentors to mentees instead of allowing them to volunteer. They picked the most talented employee in research, who reluctantly agreed to act as a mentor. However, the mentee found that his mentor was usually inaccessible and rarely spent time with him. The programme co-ordinators were reluctant to assign the mentee to another person for fear of offending his mentor. Trapped by the company politics, the mentee felt his career was being sacrificed to cover up the mistakes of senior management. Not surprisingly, he left to seek his career development elsewhere.

The moral of this story is clear. Companies should choose mentors who not only can communicate their skills well but who are also actively committed to the programme. Every volunteer mentor is worth a dozen press-ganged ones. It is not necessary for the mentor to dazzle the mentee with superior knowledge and experience – he or she merely has to be able to encourage the mentee by sharing his or her own enthusiasm for the job. The mentor must be ready to invest time and effort in the relationship, so his or her interests will probably already lie in the areas of communication and interpersonal skills. The mentor must be ready to extend friendship to the mentee and be willing to let the relationship extend beyond the normal limits of a business relationship. The mentor should not participate in the programme unless he or she is willing to consider the relationship as a relatively long-term commitment.

- Allow for a 'no-fault divorce clause'.

It is standard good practice now for mentors and mentees to be required to review the progress of the relationship after two or three meetings, with a view to assessing how suited they are to each other. If the conclusion is that they are not, the mentor can help the mentee think through what sort of mentor – if any – he or she needs at this time. We now have a small number of cases of relationships that have been dissolved in such a process but that have subsequently resumed – perhaps years later – when the mentee's circumstances and needs have changed.

MUST THE MENTEE SHARE THE SAME QUALITIES AS THE MENTOR?

There is a common assertion that in order for a mentoring relationship to succeed, the mentee must have a similar personality to the mentor's. Elizabeth Alleman and her colleague Isadore Newman (Alleman *et al*, 1984) attempted to establish whether a similarity of personality or background was indeed the basis of rewarding mentor relationships. Alleman and Newman studied 100 managers, 29 pairs reporting a mentoring relationship and 21 pairs reporting a typical business relationship. The two compared the relationship between the mentor and the mentee to the relationship between a manager and his or her superior. Through personality tests and questionnaires they discovered:

- Mentoring pairs have no more similarities in personality or background than non-mentored pairs. When participants described themselves and their partners, their profiles contained few shared traits.

- Mentoring relationships are not based on complementary personality traits. Newman and Alleman did not find evidence to support the suggestion that mentors choose mentees whose strengths and skills offset the mentor's weaknesses.

- Mentors do not believe there are any special similarities between themselves and their mentees.

- Mentees view their mentors as similar to ideal workers and identify with them to a greater extent than managers who have a non-mentoring relationship with their supervisor.

In short, Alleman and Newman demonstrate that it is not essential for the mentor and mentee to have similar personalities or backgrounds. Indeed, as we have seen, if a cultural readjustment is needed in the organisation, then it may pay to avoid deliberately too close a match.

In another more recent study of personality and mentoring, Engström (1997/1998) examined 30 pairs of mentors and mentees within a Swedish multinational company. The pairs included all gender options except female to female. He based his analysis of personality on five factors, which he describes as 'generally accepted in the field of personality and [which] include most other personality factors presented in the field'. These are: extroversion, emotional stability, agreeableness, conscientiousness and openness to experience.

Among Engström's conclusions are that mentoring relationships are seen as most successful when:

- both mentor and mentee demonstrate high extroversion

- both demonstrate a high level of agreeableness (defined as encompassing likeability, friendliness, social adaptability, altruism, affection, compliance)

- the mentee demonstrates much greater conscientiousness than the mentor (ie the mentee assumes ownership of the process)

- in the mentee's perception, the mentee demonstrates high openness to experience and the mentor high emotional stability.

An unexpected conclusion from his research was that men-only mentoring pairs were always perceived by both parties as more successful than mixed gender pairs, whether the woman was mentor or mentee. (Without a female to female comparison, this conclusion should be treated with some caution, insofar as drawing any implications is concerned.)

SUMMARY

It is remarkable how easily people in mentoring relationships develop a high level of rapport when they have a clear understanding of what they are trying to achieve together and what behaviours they should expect of each other. The key appears to be achieving the right balance of challenge and rapport between mentor and mentee.

In the next chapter, we look at the structure of the mentoring programme and the requirements of its co-ordinator.

7

Setting up the mentoring programme

Some form of spontaneous mentoring takes place in most organisations, whether acknowledged or not. A formalised programme helps harness it to the organisation's objectives. Properly managed, the programme can enhance the benefits to individuals from informal mentoring and minimise the problems that arise when the informal system bypasses talented employees.

There are usually four people involved in a mentoring programme. Together, they make up a mentoring quadrangle (see Figure 11):

- the mentee
- the mentor
- the line manager
- the programme co-ordinator, who monitors the relationships and looks at resources for training opportunities.

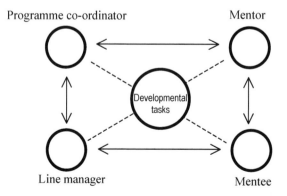

*Figure 11 | **The mentoring quadrangle***

The clearer all four are about the objectives and effort required, the more successful the programme will be. All must be involved and consulted about career moves and developmental tasks that will take the mentee away from day-to-day work and responsibilities.

Each organisation has to draw up a mentoring programme that fits its particular company culture and answers the needs of its own employees. To ensure the success of the mentoring programme, a company must be prepared to be flexible in its approach and be willing to assess continuously and, if necessary, modify the methods it has implemented.

The starting-point, as with any major corporate programme, must be a clear statement of objectives against which progress may be measured. Typical objectives might be:

- to establish a cadre of broadly trained generalist managers at or just below middle management

- to speed and improve the induction of specific types of recruits and reduce wastage within the first year of their employment

- to allow top management to assess the ability of both individual young managers and the rising generation of managers as a whole

- to provide equal opportunities for disadvantaged groups of employees.

In each case, the personnel department can establish with top management a set of assessment criteria and a timetable for achieving specific levels of results.

Putting these objectives into practice requires a great deal of preparation. Usually at least six months to a year is needed to gain acceptance of the concept from the key people in the organisation, to establish objectives and measurements, to design supporting facilities, such as special training courses, and to begin the process of selecting participants.

Throughout this process, the following principles are essential to bear in mind:

- understand how the culture of the organisation will support or hinder mentoring

- ensure top management commitment

- adapt the programme to the company's development programme

- ensure commitment and participation from mentor/mentee groups

- ensure that support systems are in place

- ensure an acceptance of the time involved

- demystify the mentoring programme

- ensure confidentiality

- measure both processes and outcomes (see Chapter 8).

PREPARING THE COMPANY FOR A MENTORING PROGRAMME

How supportive is the organisational context?

An important element in designing the programme, especially in terms of the training provision and communication within the organisation, is to understand just how supportive the environment will be towards mentoring. How will mentors and mentees be perceived?

Will line managers willingly let them spend time in mentoring meetings? Are there any cultural factors, that might inhibit mentees from using the relationship appropriately?

I often use the Development Context Survey (copies of the survey can be obtained from info@clutterbuckassociates.co.uk), a generalised indicator of how positive or negative the organisational environment is towards developmental activities, along with structured interviews with potential or actual stakeholders in the programme. Whatever process they decide to use, programme co-ordinators need to gather as much insight as possible into what will enhance or undermine mentoring.

Some examples that illustrate the point include:

- A large UK-based financial services organisation found that its system of billable hours placed a major potential barrier in the way of mentors and mentees because they would effectively be penalised for spending time on the relationship during official working hours. The solution was to produce a budget line specifically for time spent on the programme and to ensure that line managers understood the importance of making this available.

- The HR function in a UK national institution insisted that it knew exactly what the likely concerns of mentors and mentees would be and saw no need to conduct any research prior to training. Subsequently, it became very clear that the organisational culture made it difficult for the mentees – newly recruited graduates – to admit that they had any issues to deal with. They soon learned that projecting confidence and competence was essential if their appointment was to be confirmed at the end of their two-year induction. The mentees also felt that senior managers, from whom the mentors were drawn, were remote and unapproachable, so they were reluctant to disturb them with any problems they did have. The net result was that most relationships never really took off.

- An engineering company assumed that women managers would welcome a mentoring programme aimed specifically at them. Persuaded to do some initial research, it discovered that many of the women felt that labelling the programme as a women's initiative would devalue it, and that they would be less likely to take part.

Ensure top management commitment

The top management team needs to supply decisive leadership to demonstrate to the rest of the company that it considers mentoring to be a legitimate and effective method of developing and improving staff potential. Top management must support the programme verbally and materially. It must promote mentoring within the company, through speeches, letters, memoranda and articles in the company newsletter. Articles in the public media can reinforce the message greatly, because employees often take greater note of information they read in independent newspapers and magazines than they do of the same information presented in official company publications. Senior management can also attend general meetings of groups of mentoring pairs. These strategies are especially necessary if general unease, confusion, or even suspicion about the programme exists in the company.

Adapt the programme to the company's development programme

Try to fit the mentoring programme into the context of a wider framework of employee development and human resource management, and explain this framework to employees. Problems are likely to arise if the programme exists in isolation. If it seems that mentoring is the only form of career development in the company, employees may easily assume that those chosen to participate are destined automatically for senior management. The company could be accused of having a promotion system based solely on favouritism. The morale of those not on the programme would suffer appreciably. Those individuals who are on the programme may be encouraged to believe that all their chances of promotion lie in the mentoring relationship. As a result they may throw all their efforts into that area and neglect other aspects of their work. To avoid these pitfalls, mentoring should be seen as only one dimension of career development.

The company should also make sure that mentees have other opportunities to improve their skills beyond those arising within the mentoring programme. They should have access to internal or external workshops, self-development and distance-learning materials, as well as career development classes. This is to ensure that mentees can easily supplement their knowledge if the mentor's coaching is too specialised or fails to be sufficiently relevant and helpful. If the mentee is forced to rely solely on an inefficient mentor, he or she can feel frustrated and limited by the relationship. For people from disenfranchised groups and/or minorities, the company may wish in addition to make available some form of assertiveness training. At a recent round-table discussion in Washington (at the Linkage Coaching and Mentoring Conference, July 2001), the point was made quite strongly by some participants that in order to participate fully in mixed-gender mentoring training, or in cross-gender mentoring relationships, many women benefited from help in learning how to put their own views and perceptions more forcefully.

Ensure commitment and participation

Ensure that participation is voluntary. Mentoring demands time and effort, so the essential ingredient is commitment. When a company requests staff to volunteer to be mentors, it should make sure that it emphasises how demanding the relationship is. The programme co-ordinator should talk to all mentor applicants before making the final decision. If an assessment centre approach is used to select mentees, consideration should be given to designing an assessment centre for mentors, too.

Potential mentors should be informed of problems and challenges and what they should expect of the relationship. Some companies give all new mentors and mentees the chance to hear from existing mentors of the pitfalls and pleasures mentoring can bring. They also explore the mentee's view through the eyes of previous participants. The co-ordinator should also attempt to discover any ambivalence the mentor may feel about his or her commitment.

Ensure that support systems are in place

The most important of the support systems required are:

- clear information about the purpose of the programme and who is eligible for it

- some basic information about mentoring and how to apply for the programme – the Department for Employment and Education, for example, has an extensive website on its intranet

- a systematic, transparent system for matching mentors and mentees – the European Mentoring Centre can provide up-to-date information on software available

- a well-focused training programme for both mentor and mentee

- some form of mutual support mechanism by which mentors can meet from time to time to share experience and receive further advice (along the lines of supervision in counselling, although not necessarily so structured); at London Borough of Ealing, mentors meet in small groups with an experienced facilitator and mentor trainer who works with them and helps them learn from the issues they have encountered as mentors.

Some companies, such as Procter & Gamble, have supported diversity mentoring schemes with newsletters and discussion sheets aimed at stimulating dialogue between mentor and mentee. Other companies feel that most people will rapidly establish their own agenda.

Ensure an acceptance of the time involved

Make sure that everyone understands the amount of time commitment involved. As part of the preparation of the mentor, the mentee and the mentee's manager must be devoted to establishing just how much of each person's time will be taken up by the scheme. This time has to be planned for, regular meetings scheduled and a timetable established for any project work agreed.

Two key questions that must be asked are:

- How disruptive to the normal work of these people will the time commitment be?

- How valuable will this time and effort be in achieving the objective of developing the mentee?

Two useful ground rules help to put the time issue into perspective:

- If you meet less than once a quarter, you do not have a relationship (it is just an acquaintance); if you meet much more than once a month, the mentor is probably doing the line manager's job.

- Ideally, meetings should last 60–90 minutes. Less than this, it is difficult to address issues in real depth. More than two hours and you are probably going round the houses. It can be good practice to put an extra half-hour into the diary to allow for those occasions when a really crucial issue comes to the surface towards the end of the scheduled time.

Demystify the mentoring programme

Demystify the mentoring programme for those who are not involved. The methods and objectives of the programme should be explained clearly, setting out and emphasising the benefits to the organisation as a whole. If it is decided to establish only a small number of mentoring pairs as a pilot at the beginning of a programme, the organisation should explain to applicants not included that they will have an opportunity to reapply in the future.

Ensure confidentiality

Confidentiality is essential if the mentee is to open up to the mentor to produce the kind of frank relationship necessary for success. BP Chemicals ensures that all exchanges are covered by a rule of confidentiality so that the mentee can speak to the mentor as a trusted friend. One mentor comments:

The mentor should be completely aside from the line of work. It is important that total honesty and openness can be displayed, and often mentees feel wary if they do not have the distance they would like.

Confidentiality in mentoring is rarely absolute. Leaving aside the issue of legal obligations (eg becoming an accessory after the fact), different organisations have different expectations of the level of confidentiality that can apply. At the Audit Commission, the mentor is obliged to report any indication of financial misconduct, for example. At a City financial services company, top management has been careful to draw the distinction between privacy (being able to talk about issues in a relationship of trust) and confidentiality (the expectation that nothing said can be discussed outside the relationship without mutual agreement).

Clearly, the less confidence the mentee (let alone the mentor) has that what he or she says will remain between them alone, the more reluctant the mentee will be in speaking openly of his or her feelings and concerns. Said one mentee recently:

My line manager and my mentor play golf together every Sunday. There are things I'd like to explore with the mentor about how to tackle some of my manager's behaviours, but I'm never sure how much I dare say. If my manager thought I was criticising him behind his back, I'd have a real problem. As it is, twice now they have both made much the same suggestion to me about an issue I've brought up, which makes me suspicious that they have been discussing me.

Although issues of broken confidentiality are remarkably rare in mentoring, concerns over confidentiality remain one of the biggest limiting factors on relationships. Making the ground rules clear and trying, wherever possible, to avoid mentor and line manager being too close operationally or personally, are obvious practical measures to take.

Some of the engineering institutes have used mentoring for years as a means of assisting people on their route to chartered engineer. Most expected the mentor to carry out some form of assessment of the mentee, but this practice is gradually being dropped, not least because it introduced a dynamic into the relationship that made it difficult for the mentee to seek anything but technical advice – much of which was more readily available from other sources. To enrich the relationships and help build rounded professionals, the Institute of Electrical Engineers has largely divorced the measurement processes from the mentoring process.

HOW TO PREPARE THE MENTOR AND THE MENTEE

It is essential to supply as much information as possible to the two most important participants of the programme – the mentor and the mentee – for both need to understand the purpose and objectives of the programme for the individual and for the company. Both also need to understand what is expected of them. The advantages of the relationship to both the mentor and the mentee should be particularly emphasised.

The mentor

The most important aim in the preparatory stage of the programme is to motivate the mentor and help him or her see how he or she can contribute to the mentee's development.

Training

An organisation can run workshops for the mentor suggesting various methods of 'helping to learn'. A series of sessions might deal with:

- the purpose of the programme
- the benefits of the mentoring relationship
- something about mentoring
- the dynamic nature of the relationship, its stages and phases
- the core qualities and skills of an effective mentor
- practical tools and techniques for helping the mentee
- anticipating and forestalling possible problems
- adapting mentoring practices to particular settings.

It would also provide opportunities to put the skills into practice, through role-play or through tackling real issues in a one-off mentoring environment.

These workshops could operate through brainstorming sessions as well as role-play and critique sessions so that mentors can assist each other to develop greater skills. The sessions would also encourage mentors to act as a support network for each other. Typically, in the UK, the mentor training workshops last one to two days and focus both on building awareness of the role and on raising awareness of key mentoring skills. In practice, however, many organisations now insist that initial training be carried out in much shorter periods. This poses a real challenge for the trainer, who must not only ensure that mentors emerge from less than half a day's training with enough understanding and confidence to try being a mentor, but must also find innovative ways of encouraging them to come back to review their progress. One current programme in the City is building in time for an external coach to sit in on mentoring sessions and provide mentors with a one-to-one briefing on their approach.

British American Tobacco (BAT) adopted a very flexible approach when it designed its international graduate mentoring programme. First, it linked together mentoring and coaching as parallel programmes, training managers in both skills, and training mentees in what to expect from the immediate line manager in the form of coaching and from the off-line mentor. The programmes were encapsulated in ring-binders available to all workshop participants. To customise the programme to the varying requirements of its subsidiaries around the world, the training manuals were designed to be recast as needed into one-day, one-and-a-half-day and two-day versions. The case studies were also replaceable, as needed, with local examples more suited to the national culture. Trainers from around the world were trained as facilitators with authority to adapt the materials to local circumstances. (Some had participated in the original design, as well, to make sure it met a wide range of needs.)

Is it possible to do without training at all? Practical experience suggests that this usually results in a high proportion of failed relationships and severe damage to the concept of mentoring within the organisation. A rough-and-ready rule of thumb is that programmes introduced without any training, or with a minimalist briefing, rarely result in more than one in three relationships delivering any significant benefits to the participants. The fact that any relationships work at all seems to relate to the previous experience of mentoring by the people concerned and to the innate and instinctive competence some people have in the mentoring role. Training the mentor can double the success rate to 6 out of 10; training mentor and mentee, plus ensuring that the line managers also understand the purpose of the scheme and its benefits to them, pushes the success rate to over 90 per cent.

Examine risks

Organisations can help the mentor to examine frankly the potential risks involved in being a mentor. Programme co-ordinators should make it clear to the mentor and the company in general that the relationship is not guaranteed to be successful and that a failed pairing will not reflect badly on the mentor. Indeed, having the self-confidence to wind down a relationship that is not going anywhere should be seen as a sign of the mentor's developmental competence.

Cross-gender relationships

Alert 'cross-gender' mentors to the potential problems. The discovery that rumour and sexual innuendo exists about a mentoring couple can decisively restrict or even destroy the relationship.

If the two parties are forewarned, they can cope with the external pressures better or adopt strategies to avoid giving encouragement to rumour.

Networking

Introduce the mentor to other managers who have experience in mentoring and who can discuss the various stages of the relationship and the challenges and difficulties that are likely to arise. Organisations can also appoint a senior or 'super' mentor to counsel and guide the less experienced mentor.

Online training

If appropriate, the company can provide training on demand using e-learning. There is a growing variety of resources here, and at least one UK company is introducing its own e-learning programme in mentoring independently.

Mentoring certificate

For some people, the opportunity to obtain a certificate is attractive. The National Standards in Mentoring document issued in 2000 after piloting with 300 organisations, from companies to schools, is intended eventually to form the basis of a mentoring NVQ, and other formal qualifications are starting to appear. Great care should be exercised in determining the value and validity of some of these diplomas and certificates, a number of which seem to have only marginal relevance to mentoring.

The mentee

If the mentee is to take appropriate responsibility for the relationship, he or she must understand:

- what the organisation expects from the programme
- what can realistically be expected of the mentor
- what the mentor should expect of him or her
- what he or she can do to make the relationship deliver positive outcomes for both parties.

In most of the programmes that I have worked on over the past five years, the style of the mentee training depends very much on the maturity of the target audience. Young people in community schemes, ex-offenders and recent graduate recruits tend to be trained in a peer group. People at more senior level, or who are generally more experienced, tend to be included in a mixed group with mentors. The rationale behind this is first that mentor and mentee will manage the relationship better if they appreciate how it appears from the other side, and second that mentors can improve their skills if they also become mentees, and mentees if they in turn act as mentors. Incorporating role-swaps into the training encourages insight into appropriate behaviours and helps build the kind of openness under which the relationship will flourish. Although it does sometimes happen that an intended mentoring pair train together, training usually occurs before matching takes place – so this provides another opportunity for the mentee to vet some potential mentors.

An additional element I have introduced into many mentee training workshops is a more intensive session on building and using networks. The more adept the mentee becomes at using networking, the more helpful the mentor can be. A good starting-point for developing learning nets is the peer group, which may have all the knowledge the graduate mentee needs to gain introductions to areas of the business he or she would like to know about. Similarly, some skills in career self-management come in very useful.

At a more senior level, the scheme co-ordinator may spend time helping mentees think through the nature of the transition they would like to make and how exactly they think a mentor can help. This both assists in the selection phase and ensures that the relationship can get started with a relatively clear sense of purpose.

GETTING STARTED

Although a handful of companies start the whole process with a meeting at which the line manager or the scheme co-ordinator facilitates, in general this is perceived to be unnecessarily intrusive. Instead, mentor and mentee are usually encouraged to meet at a mutually convenient and not too formal place to work out on their own how they want to run their relationship. However, the primary objective of the first meeting is to get to know each other and build the rapport they will need to make the relationship work.

At this or the next meeting, the mentee should also be prepared to share with the mentor any information he or she has that is relevant to issues he or she wants to work on – for example, performance appraisals, assessment centre results or the outcomes of psychometric tests undertaken. I often ask my mentees to record once a week or so the three things that have most pleased and most frustrated them. Then either we examine the list together, to look for patterns, or the mentees extract their own meaning from the list before we meet. In this way, the dialogue becomes grounded in actual, recent experience rather than hypotheticals. Long-term developmental goals can be illuminated through examining more recent successes and failures.

THE ROLE OF THE LINE MANAGER *V* THAT OF THE MENTOR

To avoid clashes between mentor and line manager, or worse, deliberate manipulation of them by the mentee, it is important that line manager and mentor are clear about where the boundaries of their responsibility towards the mentee lie. Table 4 attempts to distinguish between the responsibilities and indicate where the responsibility is shared. Some organisations may wish to move the responsibilities around to suit their specific circum-stances – no problem, as long as line managers and mentors are clear where they stand.

Table 4 | *Development roles of line manager and mentor*

Line manager	Shared	Mentor
Performance appraisal	Encouragement, motivation to learn	Help learner develop insights into causes of poor performance
Agreed developmental goals within learner's current job	Shape goals beyond current job	Help learner manage the integration of job, career and personal goals
Help learner build relationships within the team	Help learner build relationships outside the team	Help learner build relationships with line manager
Find opportunities to stretch learner's performance	Find opportunities to stretch learner's thinking	Challenge learner's thinking and assumptions
Give constructive feedback through observation	Help learner develop skills of intrinsic observation	Help learner accept and manage feedback constructively
Role model for task fulfilment and growth	Role model of general behaviour	Role model for personal achievement and growth

TESTING THE PROGRAMME

Start in a modest way to make sure that the initial effort is well designed and fulfils its objectives. Once a trial programme, involving say 5–20 mentoring pairs, has been successfully established, the company can decide to be more ambitious and expand its size and timescale. In this way the organisation can avoid most of the disillusionment and backlash that can come when a full-blown programme fails to live up to its objectives.

The key questions in designing the training support for a mentoring programme are:

- Who should be trained?
- How much training is needed?
- Should mentor and mentee be trained together or separately?
- What makes for quality of training?
- When and how should training be delivered?

Who should be trained?

The basic statistics of training in mentoring appear roughly to be:

- Do not train or brief any of the participants – expect 10 per cent of relationships to deliver significant learning for one or both parties. (That is the baseline of people who have had previous exposure to effective mentoring or who have a very strong instinctive capability.)

- Rely on a briefing only – expect 30 per cent of relationships to succeed. (That is the proportion of mentors who will extrapolate from other situations and training to lock into the role.)

- Train mentors but not mentees – expect up to 60 per cent of relationships to deliver learning for mentors and perhaps half as many to deliver learning for the mentees. (Mentees will typically fail to take over the management of the relationship and will not fully appreciate their own and their mentors' roles.)

- Train both mentors and mentees – expect 90 per cent plus of relationships to deliver significant learning for both parties, especially when line managers are also well briefed and informed in general about the programme.

It also helps if the steering group and/or scheme co-ordinator have attended a workshop aimed at broadening their understanding of mentoring concept and good practice.

How much training is needed?

The answer here is that it depends on the level at which mentoring is to take place. If the mentor is to be a professional working with, say, executives or young offenders, an extensive period of theoretical learning and practice is essential. (See Chapter 5 on competencies for a longer examination of this issue.) For the manager in a workplace, however, the basic need is for enough understanding and skill to respond appropriately to the mentee's needs for guidance, help in thinking issues through and general support, and to know where the boundaries of his or her competence lie (and hence to refer on to specialist support if needed).

Realistically, this cannot be done in less than a day. Moreover, experience indicates time and again that a single sheep-dip event is not enough. To sustain the programme, mentors need to come back together again at least once over the following six to eight months to review what they have learned, to identify problem areas, and to be equipped with additional techniques relevant to the situations they have encountered.

Extracting sufficient time for mentor training is almost always a problem. Particularly at senior management levels, people often think they already have the skills. What this often means is that they have attended a coaching course at some time in the past, but do not understand the difference between the two approaches. The reality is that the more senior people are, the less effective they may be at listening and the more reliant on giving advice. Some of the approaches we have taken to overcome senior manager reluctance to invest properly in training include:

- adapting the content to emphasise advanced developmental techniques and the role of mentoring in shaping future leaders

- giving top managers individual, customised one-to-one training sessions, both to get started and to review their experiences in the mentor role

- breaking up the initial training into two-hour chunks.

Mentee training is usually easier to arrange, especially when the mentees are relatively junior in the organisation. Some organisations have skimped here, opting instead for a briefing, in the mistaken belief that the mentees' role is relatively passive. In reality the mentees need to have as broad an understanding of the process as the mentor. They also need to acquire a portfolio of skills to manage the relationship and to help the mentor help them.

Should mentor and mentee be trained together or separately?

(*This section is extracted from an article by David Clutterbuck and Jenny Sweeney, 'Apart or together: good practice in training mentors and mentees', published in the Clutterbuck Associates newsletter, September 2003.*)

One of the most difficult and contentious questions we encounter in helping organisations design and implement mentoring schemes is whether to conduct the training for the two groups separately or together. There is no generic right answer and our experience covers both options. Yet getting this aspect of it right can make or break a programme, and we have seen a number of examples of failure where it has been badly managed.

The starting-point for the scheme co-ordinator in considering this issue is that both mentors and mentees need to undergo some training if the majority of relationships are going to deliver significant benefits. The quality and quantity of mutual learning and the proportion of relationships seen by both parties as successful is greatly enhanced with appropriate initial training. Bringing participant groups back together again to review experience and receive additional ad hoc training as needed also improves the success rate.

Within the initial training, the critical elements for both mentors and mentees are:

- gaining a complementary understanding of how to manage the relationship – the roles, responsibilities and expected behaviours – and how it should evolve over time

- learning the skills of being an effective mentor/mentee. Our observation is that the mentees are best able to help the mentor help them, if they understand the processes/techniques the mentor is using and can collaborate in making those processes work.

In both elements, an appreciation of the other party's perspective is going to be very helpful, if not essential, in getting the most out of the relationship. But whether that need is best addressed through joint or separate training events depends very much on circumstance.

Let's look at the arguments for each approach, with some examples of positive and negative experience.

The case for training together

Certain situations make it quite difficult to separate out mentors from mentees. For example, at a pharmaceutical company, people who came to the initial workshops did not know whether they wanted to be a mentor or a mentee. In practice, people who came with one role in mind often decided they would best adopt the other – and some adopted both.

Another situation in which joint training is common occurs in cascade mentoring programmes: where several layers of employees are being mentored by those above, many of the participants end up playing both roles, within different relationships.

An important consideration in the success of a programme is ensuring that both mentor and mentee receive appropriate training as soon as possible after they are selected for inclusion. One programme ran into severe problems because the time gap between training of mentors and training of mentees gradually extended until many of the participants simply lost interest.

A third factor in favour of training together is that it provides a valuable opportunity to experience the other side's perspective directly. An illustration of what happens when one or both parties does not understand the other's perspective comes from a large and venerable financial institution. The programme failed because mentees did not really believe that mentors were approachable and willing to discuss a wide range of developmental topics. Their observations about the organisation's culture ('Sort your own problems.' 'Don't complain.' 'Never admit any weaknesses.') got in the way because they had never heard the mentors – either individually or as a group – commit to the different agenda.

There are other ways to share perspectives and expectations – for example, a number of companies co-opt mentors from the previous year's programme to talk to mentees about their experience, and vice versa – but it is difficult to create the same level of understanding as comes from the immediate and intuitive responses of a number of mentors or mentees together. BP, which introduced an upward mentoring programme – in which junior people of different race and/or gender become mutual mentors to senior managers – opted to train both together because it needed to build initial confidence among mentees that senior managers were genuinely committed to open dialogue on diversity issues. In such circumstances, there is no real substitute for hearing it direct.

CASE STUDY

A government department with offices across the world

The programme is designed to be open and self-selecting. Mentees use a website to select a mentor from a pool of volunteers, but not everyone is sure at the beginning which role he or she will take. For this reason – and to manage the numbers, so that training can be on offer as soon as possible after a pairing is made – the practical solution was to train both together. Those people who are sure they want to become mentees usually find particular value in skills training, because it helps them get more out of the programme and their mentors.

CASE STUDY

The Acquisition Leadership Development Scheme (ALDS)

This programme draws its participants from military and civilian employees in the three armed services of the UK and is part of a larger leadership development programme. Each year the intake of 100 participants (mentors and mentees) attend mentoring training in groups of 25. The wide range of levels and backgrounds from which participants come allows almost everyone attending the training to find a mentor, mentee, or both, within the 100-strong cohort. Some find it useful to pair with members of earlier cohorts.

The case for training apart

The case for training apart is equally strong, and equally dependent on circumstances. Most commonly, it occurs in relatively traditional programmes in which mentors and mentees have already been selected, although they may or may not have been matched.

Among the arguments for separate training are:

- It enables mentors and mentees to be open about their hopes and fears for the programme. Typical fears among mentors relate to whether they are really capable of doing the role well. Among mentees there may be concerns about confidentiality, or about why they have been selected to take part. (For example: 'Is there really a hidden remedial agenda?') The point is illustrated by the following quote from a mentee in a major chemicals business when the mentees as a group were offered the chance to merge their training with a mentor group:

I've got to know one mentor very well and I'm very open with him. That doesn't mean I see all the other mentors in the same light – they are still senior managers to me. My behaviour would revert to normal in that group, which would make me feel false in the relationship with my own mentor.

  In cultures that are not very positive towards developmental behaviours and where mentoring and coaching are not seen as natural to everyday management, such concerns will be particularly influential on the success of the programme. By contrast, organisations with very positive developmental cultures may well find that people prefer to be trained together because it is one more opportunity to learn from another group.

- It is much easier to focus the workshops around the specific needs of each group. Although much of the broad agenda for a workshop will be common, mentors need to spend more time practising skills and techniques, while mentees need more time to consider how they want to use a mentor and how they will gradually take the lead in managing the relationship.

- The difficulty of getting senior managers to commit sufficient time to training for the role. A day is generally regarded as the minimum initial training for both mentor and mentee, but if the mentors resist, then the programme co-ordinator has the choice of training separately, or trying to cram training for both into insufficient time. Training separately does not overcome the senior manager problem, but it does ensure that the mentees are adequately prepared for their roles.

So there is no right answer, but hopefully this analysis will help you decide which approach will work best for your scheme.

What makes for quality of training?

Because quality derives from 'fitness for purpose', a lot depends on the objectives of the scheme and the context in which it takes place. In mentee terms, what will suit a group of legal analysts seeking partnership is unlikely to do the job for a bunch of young offenders – and the same would be true for their respective mentors.

Key factors to take into account include:

Composition

There should be a good mix of:

- theory (most training we have evaluated is very poor on mentoring theory, although it often includes generalised management or behavioural theory)
- discussion of scheme purpose
- discussion of roles and responsibilities
- opportunity to explore one's own motives and objectives and, if possible, those of the other party
- exploration of competencies of an effective mentor and mentee
- exposure to relevant skills of relationship management
- practice of relevant skills for learning within the mentoring dyad.

Groundedness

It makes a substantial difference to people's motivation if the training sessions are attended by top management, to outline the value of the programme to the organisation and to talk about their own experiences in the mentor and/or mentee role. It is also useful to invite participants from previous schemes to discuss their experience – warts and all.

Trainer/facilitator knowledge

It adds considerably to the credibility of the workshop if the trainer is able to refer to his or her own experience as mentor and mentee. Participants also appear to value it when the facilitator is able to provide a breadth of example of good practice from other schemes, and especially from other organisations.

Matching training provision to the phases of relationship evolution

One approach that does not work is to throw all the training for mentors and mentees at them in one go. There is simply too much to absorb, and people need an opportunity to practise basic skills and techniques before they attempt more advanced ones. Broadly speaking, training interventions can best be made as they move from one phase of the relationship to the next. (See Chapter 11 for a more detailed description of the phases.)

At the initiation phase of the relationship, mentors and mentees must understand the purpose of the programme, how to build rapport and how to begin to set goals and boundaries for the relationship. A few months later, they need the skills to review progress and sharpen up personal goals. They also typically value an opportunity to refresh their understanding of the basics. Some months later again – by which time they should be in the progress-making phase – they will appreciate more advanced skills of drawing out and exploring issues. One very successful scheme, for example, instructs participants in emotional intelligence at this point. Finally, both mentor and mentee must be prepared for a positive winding up of the relationship, and they usually value an opportunity to discuss how best to accomplish that.

Some organisations, especially corporations in the United States with very large mentoring programmes, have established monthly lunch or breakfast seminars aimed at providing continuous development for mentors and mentees. Other organisations have opted for an initial intensive one-day introduction to mentoring, followed by two or three one- or two-day further development sessions. The aim, in both cases, is to maintain a steady pace of process learning for both mentor and mentee.

Putting training and scheme management together

The chart on the next page (Table 5) is an example of how the scheme management and training processes can be integrated over a one-year programme. It is not intended to be a fixed template – merely an illustration of what a well-planned programme might involve.

*Table 5 | **Integration of scheme management and training processes***

Training intervention	Mentor development	Mentee development
Rapport-building/ direction-setting *Communication with sponsors:* Programme objectives and expected benefits Results of initial survey of participants Results of development climate survey, if used	*Skills:* Understanding of mentoring process and roles Introduction to reflective space Relationship development and management (including boundary management) Questioning/listening techniques Goal-setting Managing intrinsic feedback Double-loop learning processes *Measurement:* Training effectiveness Relationship expectations (Dynamics survey, Part 1)	*Skills:* Understanding of mentoring process and roles Introduction to reflective space Relationship development and management (including boundary management) Goal-setting Managing intrinsic feedback Double-loop learning processes *Measurement:* Training effectiveness Relationship expectations (Dynamics survey, Part 1)
Initial review *Communication with sponsors:* Results of Dynamics survey, Part 2 Meet the participants session	*Skills:* Informal relationship review processes (how are we doing?) Using anecdote and story Triple-loop learning processes The mentor as networker/ link to resources The mentor as career counsellor/workplace counsellor *Sustaining interest:* Newsletter 1 *Measurement:* Dynamics survey, Part 2	*Skills:* Career self-management How to pose and pursue issues for discussion Managing the learning net *Sustaining interest:* Newsletter 1 *Measurement:* Dynamics survey, Part 2

Secondary review	*Skills:* Managing constructive challenge and confrontation The mentor as guardian The mentor as coach Understanding and using emotional intelligence	*Skills:* Managing constructive challenge and confrontation
Communication with sponsors: Results of Dynamics survey, Part 3 Developers' Council	*Sustaining interest:* Newsletter 3 Developer's Council *Measurement:* Dynamics survey, Part 3	*Sustaining interest:* Newsletter 3 *Measurement:* Dynamics survey, Part 3
Winding-up review	*Skills:* How to move beyond the formal relationship Formal learning review Becoming a mentee – whether, when and how Further (advanced) techniques and approaches	*Skills:* How to move beyond the formal relationship Formal learning review Becoming a mentor – whether, when and how
Communication with sponsors: Plans for next phases of the programme/new target groups Report of balanced scorecard survey	*Sustaining interest:* Developers' Council *Measurement:* Balanced scorecard Mentoring scheme standards	*Sustaining interest:* Alumni group *Measurement:* Balanced scorecard Mentoring scheme standards

Explanations

Alumni group – one or two of the mentees agree to manage a monthly chatroom for their colleagues. Each new wave of mentees is invited to participate.

Balanced scorecard – a survey method that assesses the programme against four elements:

- relationship processes
- relationship outcomes
- programme processes
- programme outcomes.

Developers' Council – mentors are recognised for their role as developers. They meet with top management periodically to discuss the broader issues of talent management and people development. In this way they become part of the strategic thinking of the organisation with regard to people issues.

Dynamics survey – a three-part survey measuring expectations of the relationship, behaviours within it and outcomes for both mentor and mentee.

Newsletter – a summary of what individual pairs are doing; tips and techniques; questions asked on the hot line or addressed to the programme co-ordinator.

SUMMARY

To be really successful, a mentoring programme must obtain acceptance and commitment from participants and non-participants alike. The scheme should have empathetic, carefully selected and trained mentors and mentees who understand how to make the most of opportunities, and clear goals accepted by all. A great deal of effort is therefore needed to prepare employees at all levels for the introduction of the programme, ensuring that everyone knows what is happening, why and how the scheme will work. Particular attention should be given to the mentoring pairs, the mentee's boss and the mentee's peers. Starting small with a modest experiment helps take some of the bugs out of the system before it is applied generally throughout the organisation.

Part 3:

Managing mentoring programmes and relationships

8

Beginning the mentoring relationship

The relationship should develop swiftly and smoothly if both mentor and mentee have been well matched and well prepared. The phases the relationship typically goes through are examined in the next chapter. In this short section we look at how to make sure that the mentoring pair make the most of the opportunity given them.

By the time the mentor and mentee hold their first formal meeting under the mentoring programme, both should have a clear idea of the objectives of the relationship. These may be relatively vague at this stage, not least because the programme is intended to help the mentee refine and develop his or her career objectives. However, it should at least start with some form of assessment of the mentee's strengths and weaknesses, the nature of the transition he or she would like to make, and what the longer-term ambitions are. It will also, of course, take into account the general programme objectives, which both parties should understand clearly.

Typical starting objectives might include:

- Introduce the mentee to other, parallel functions or departments whose work he or she will need to understand to progress or that may open his or her eyes to potential sideways moves.

- Help the mentee break down a seemingly impossible or far-fetched goal into a series of more tangible tasks that he or she can begin to address. Having a more or less detailed route-map of the experience, skills and competencies he or she needs to gather, the mentee can enter on to a self-development or career management path with greater confidence and commitment.

- Help the mentee think through how to raise his or her visibility where it matters.

- Help the mentee establish the informal networks he or she needs to be effective in the organisation.

- Act as a sounding-board in helping the mentee work out how to manage difficult relationships with working colleagues.

- Help the mentee think through how to apply in practice what he or she is learning through theoretical study.

- Gain a real understanding of the career choices that face the mentee, and the implications of each choice.

Some organisations prefer to set out objectives in terms of process rather than outcomes. For example, a large UK chemical company sets out the following responsibilities at the beginning of a mentoring relationship:

- Meet the mentee once a month for at least an hour by timetabling formally in advance.

- Ensure that the mentee maintains a brief diary of daily events to form the basis for the monthly discussion.

- Develop a personal relationship with the mentee.

- Maintain the relationship for two years.

The objectives will be defined and adopted as the relationship develops and as the mentee's needs change. It is also expected that the two people start off with the same understanding of the ground rules of the relationship. In particular, there have to be clear rules of behaviour.

Another common guideline is: 'The mentor will only communicate his or her knowledge of the mentee to other parties with the mentee's consent.'

A more detailed and generic code of practice for the mentoring relationship is that designed for the National Standards, and is reproduced in the box below. Some organisations provide a general set of core rules for all mentoring relationships; others leave it to the individuals to decide. Whichever route they choose, the aim is to help the mentee stand on his or her own feet, not to make him or her dependent.

An ethical code of practice for mentoring

- The mentor's role is to respond to the mentee's developmental needs and agenda; it is not to impose his or her own agenda.

- Mentors must work within the current agreement with the mentee about confidentiality that is appropriate within the context.

- The mentor will not intrude into areas the mentee wishes to keep private until invited to do so. However, he or she should help the mentee recognise how other issues may relate to those areas.

- Mentor and mentee should aim to be open and truthful with each other and themselves about the relationship itself.

- The mentoring relationship must not be exploitative in any way, nor can it be open to misinterpretation.

- Mentors need to be aware of the limits of their own competence and operate within these limits.

- Mentors have a responsibility to develop their own competence in the practice of mentoring.

- The mentee must accept increasing responsibility for managing the relationship; the mentor should empower them to do so and must generally promote the mentee's autonomy.

- Mentor and mentee should respect each other's time and other responsibilities, ensuring that they do not impose beyond what is reasonable.

- Mentor and mentee share responsibility for the smooth winding down of the relationship when it has achieved its purpose – they must both avoid creating dependency.

- Either party may dissolve the relationship. However, both mentor and mentee have a responsibility for discussing the matter together as part of mutual learning.

- The mentee should be aware of his or her rights and any complaints procedures.

- Mentors must be aware of any current law and work within the law.

- Mentor and mentee must be aware that all records are subject to statutory regulations under the Data Protection Act 1998.

MEASURING AND MONITORING THE PROGRAMME

The company also needs some system of feedback and evaluation in order to know whether mentoring is functioning efficiently and successfully. For example, one large UK manufacturing company holds a graduate workshop at least once a year so that graduate mentees can get together and produce a report recommending changes in the system.

In fact, there are three main reasons for measuring:

- to troubleshoot individual relationships

- to provide information for quality improvement of the mentoring programme

- to demonstrate to top management that the investment in mentoring has been worthwhile.

One of the paradoxes of formal mentoring programmes is that the essence of the relationship is its informality – the ability to discuss in private a wide range of issues that will help the mentee cope with and learn from issues he or she encounters, putting aside any power or status differences that might operate outside the relationship. So the idea of measurement and review is, on the face of it, to some extent at odds with the need to retain a high degree of informality and ad hoc responsiveness.

In practice, a certain amount of measurement provides the foundation on which the informal relationship can grow most healthily. It allows:

- scheme co-ordinators to recognise where additional support is needed and to improve the operation of the scheme – not least the training

- mentors and mentees to work together to build the relationship, understanding more clearly what each can and does bring to the discussions.

Where attempts to measure mentoring become unacceptable, they usually involve:

- an attempt to assess and report upon mentees' performance to a third party
- a link between the mentor's opinion and a specific reward for the mentee (a promotion or a diploma, for example) – here the role has become more that of a tutor
- disclosure of the content of discussions.

In such circumstances, measurement is likely to make the mentee – and sometimes the mentor – less open, less willing to admit weaknesses and less trusting, hence limiting the potential of the relationship to deliver high quantity and quality of learning.

By contrast effective measurement in mentoring is:

- relatively unobtrusive
- valued by all parties as helpful
- timely
- straightforward and easy to apply.

The measurement matrix

Mentoring measurements fall into four categories, illustrated in Figure 12.

*Figure 12 | **Categories of mentoring measurements***

Relationship

Programme

Processes   Outcomes

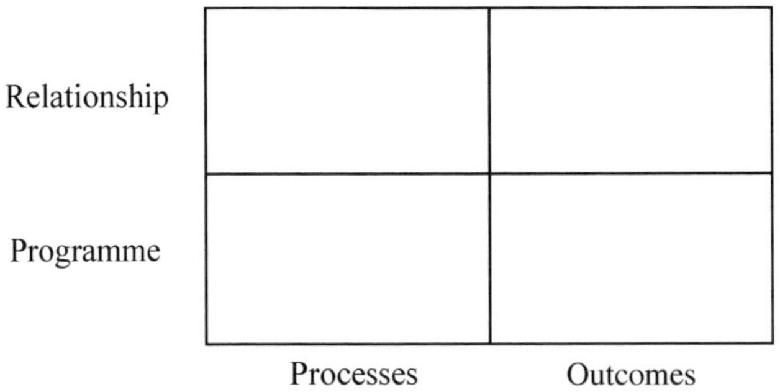

- *Relationship processes* – what happens in the relationship; for example, how often do the pair meet? Have they developed sufficient trust? Is there a clear sense of direction to the relationship? Do the mentor or the mentee have concerns about his or her own or the other person's contribution to the relationship?

- *Programme processes* – for example, how many people attended training? How effective was the training? In some cases, programme processes will also include data derived from adding together measurements from individual relationships, to gain a broad picture of what is going well and less well.

- *Relationship outcomes* – have mentor and mentee met the goals they set? (Some adjustment may be needed for legitimate changes in goals as circumstances evolve.)

- *Programme outcomes* – for example, have we increased retention of key staff, or raised the competence of the mentees in critical areas?

Measuring all four gives you a balanced view of the mentoring programme and allows the scheme co-ordinator to intervene, with sensitivity, where needed.

Table 6 shows the actual measures used by GlaxoSmithKline's finance division. The total number of measures was kept to a maximum of 10, covering the full spectrum of hard and soft measures, process and outcomes and relationship and programme measures.

*Table 6 | **Mentoring measures used by GlaxoSmithKline***

Corporate process	Corporate outcome/goals
How often: at least 5 meetings *What phase: set direction + working towards targets* *People are networking more*	*Mentee is asking for development opportunities* *Has a plan/action around raising personal profile*
Relationship process	Relationship outcomes
Do we trust each other/work together well? *Are we dealing with real issues?* *Do I enjoy it?*	*Has significant learning taken place?* *Have you gained in competence in an area you wanted to work on?*

What should be reviewed, when?

At the programme planning stage

There is a need at both programme and relationship level for a clear purpose up front and a clear idea of what behaviours are expected from both mentors and mentees. It is good practice to involve potential participants and other interested parties (eg line managers, top management) to agree measurements at the beginning. At the very least this discussion will establish the extent to which measurements can be 'soft' (qualitative) or 'hard' (quantitative).

Many organisations now begin the programme with a short research project to establish likely barriers and drivers to mentoring.

In selecting/training mentors and mentees

Mentors and mentees can benefit from greater self-awareness of their strengths and weaknesses as developers of others. Mentees often need to have some ideas about the areas of interpersonal behaviour they can work on with the mentor.

After the first few meetings

This is the opportunity for mentor and mentee to review whether the relationship is going to work. Key questions here include:

- Have we established strong rapport and trust, sufficient to work together?
- Does the mentee perceive the mentor's input as relevant and stimulating?
- If not, what sort of person does the mentee need to work with?

The scheme co-ordinator will want by this point to know whether people are meeting, and whether they have discussed the future of the relationship.

As the relationship progresses

The scheme co-ordinator will want at the minimum to know what further support is needed, if any, in the form of further, more focused skills training, or general encouragement to participants.

Good practice typically involves a short survey of participants, followed by a review session during which some ad hoc training can be provided.

At the end of the relationship

Assuming that the relationship achieves its objectives and winds down, it is useful for both parties to review the following:

- What did we expect to achieve?
- What did we actually achieve?
- What else did we learn on the way?
- How will we use what we have learned in future developmental relationships?

At the end of the programme

Assuming that the programme assigns an end to the formal mentoring relationship (many relationships will, of course, continue informally thereafter), the outcomes can be measured against the original goals.

THE MENTORING CONTRACT

The notion of a mentoring contract is widespread and poses a similar conundrum to measurement. To what extent should we risk bureaucratising an essentially informal process? Some clarity is essential, but how much, and does a written document contribute greatly to clarity anyway?

There is no straightforward answer, not least because it depends on circumstance. In an experiment some years ago within the National Health Service, I provided 100 pairs of mentors and mentees with detailed discussion guides, formal contracts to sign and extensive background notes. I then invited them to use these religiously, to scan them and put them aside, or to ignore them altogether. When we reviewed the results it became clear that only 20 per cent had completed the contracts, while the others had roughly half-and-half scanned or ditched them. The success rate of the relationships did not seem to be affected by their choice. From this I conclude that it should be left to the mentee and mentor to decide how they approach the issue of contracting.

What does seem to be essential is that both sides discuss the relationship objectives, their expectations of each other, and how they will manage the relationship. The following checklist seems to provide a basic set of questions most people can relate to in discussing these issues.

Mentoring ground rules

1   a) Are we clear about each other's expectations of:

- each other?
- the mentoring relationship?
- what we hope to learn from each other?

     b) How closely do our expectations match?

     c) How directive or non-directive should the mentor be in each meeting?

2   a) What are the core topics we want to discuss?

     b) What, if any, are the limits to the scope of discussion (ie what we talk about)?

3   Who will take primary responsibility – ie the mentor, the mentee or both together – for:

- deciding how often to meet?
- setting the agenda for meetings?
- ensuring that meetings take place?
- organising where to meet, and for how long?
- defining learning goals?
- initiating reviews of progress?

4   How formal or informal do we want our meetings to be?

5   To what extent is the mentor prepared to allow the mentee to:

- use his or her authority?
- use his or her networks?
- take up time between meetings?

6   Are we agreed that openness and trust are essential? How will we ensure that they happen?

7   Are we both willing to give honest and timely feedback (eg to be a critical friend)?

8   a) What, if any, are the limits to the confidentiality of this relationship?

b) What are we prepared to tell others:

- about the relationship?
- about our discussions?

c) Who shall we tell, and how?

9   What responsibilities do we owe to others as a result of this relationship (eg to line managers, peers, the programme co-ordinator)?

10 a) How do we ensure that the mentee's line manager is supportive?

b) Is there a clear distinction between the roles of mentor and line manager?

c) If there are overlaps, how will these be managed?

11 When and how shall we check this relationship is 'right' for both of us?

THE ROLE OF THE MENTORING CO-ORDINATOR

The task of the mentoring co-ordinator can be quite formidable.

He or she is the formal link between participants and top management, the primary source of troubleshooting for relationships in difficulty, and the person responsible for all the support mechanisms. Key activities include:

- managing the publicity for the scheme and the recruitment of mentors and mentees
- arranging initial training and follow-up
- maintaining the website, where there is one
- administering the matching process and any reassignments that are needed
- ensuring that measurement and review processes take place when they are supposed to
- managing the budgets and quality control processes

- being the public face of the programme to audiences inside and outside the organisation.

One of the most common reasons mentoring programmes falter is that there is no one with the assigned time or priorities to devote to these activities. It is therefore imperative that before the company embarks on a major expansion of mentoring, it ensures that there is sufficient management resource to support it. A rough calculation is that it requires one full day a week of an HR professional's time for every 20 mentoring pairs. Some companies with large graduate mentoring programmes ease the burden by assigning second-year graduate recruits to the HR department to absorb the bulk of the administrative burden. This is a prized assignment, as the graduate gets to know a very large slice of the organisation in the year or so he or she is attached to the project.

SUMMARY

The mentoring programme needs considerable maintenance; it cannot be left to its own devices. Monitoring of progress towards regularly reviewed objectives is essential to ensure that mentee, mentor and company all benefit from the scheme.

9

Standards for mentoring programmes

One of the clear conclusions from the experiences of hundreds of mentoring schemes is that attention to doing it well pays dividends. Failure (see Chapter 12) is almost always the result of a combination of:

- inadequate groundwork (preparing the organisation and stakeholders, having clear objectives, and so on)

- inadequate training (for both mentors and mentees, and ideally also for key third parties, such as the mentees' line managers)

- insufficient continuing support to sustain the programme.

Conversely, investment in these areas typically ensures that the programme delivers very good value for money and has a significant impact on the learning and careers of the majority of both mentors and mentees.

The need for standards for mentoring schemes is based on four factors:

- Scheme co-ordinators need some kind of pragmatic benchmark of good practice to use as a guideline in both designing and assessing their mentoring schemes.

- It is increasingly important to HR professionals to be able to demonstrate that the initiatives they have implemented on behalf of the organisation are well-designed and well-founded.

- External endorsement of a scheme, to a recognised standard, gives participants greater confidence that they will receive the quality of support they need to make the most of the mentoring opportunities.

- They provide a broad basis for measuring improvement in the quality and effectiveness of a mentoring scheme.

Our research into existing scheme standards has identified only three. Some years ago an attempt was made to introduce mentoring standards into schools in California. Schools tended to use the standards for design purposes, but relatively few formal assessments were made, primarily because of budgetary considerations. (The same would probably hold true of schools in the UK.) The National Mentoring Network, supported by the Active Community Unit at the Home Office and the Department for Education and Skills in October 2001 launched the Approved Provider Standard (APS). The APS is a national quality-approved benchmark for one-to-one volunteer mentoring schemes. Advantages of the Standard are cited as including:

- Organisations which receive approval are put through a rigorous process of competency.

- Approved organisations will receive recognition for good practice.

- The Standard will form the basis of a Government-endorsed national database of Approved Providers.

- Approved Providers will be granted the Award certificate and the use of the Approved Provider logo to help promote their programme.

The *International Standards for Mentoring Programmes in Employment*, launched in 2003 after extensive consultation with scheme co-ordinators and other observers of good practice, who advisory board I chair, are focused very closely on mentoring in the workplace. They provide a generic platform for the design and assessment of schemes for graduate recruits, diversity programmes, technical qualification programmes, and most other situations with a mixture of career and personal development objectives. They apply in a wide variety of cultures and across the worlds of commerce, manufacturing, higher education and the voluntary sector. They are currently available for assessment in Scandinavia, Australia, southern Africa, Switzerland, the Republic of Ireland, the UK, Canada, Singapore and the United States.

The *International Standards* have six sections. The first deals with the clarity of purpose of the scheme. Do all the key stakeholders understand what it aims to achieve for the organisation and for the participants? The second covers the quantity and quality of training provided. Is it sufficient to get people started with confidence and an understanding of how to learn the role by doing it? The third area covers selection and matching processes. Do mentors and mentees have a say in how they are matched? Is there an appropriate policy and approach for rematching? The fourth deals with measurement and review. Do the measures selected establish how effective the programme has been at the levels of both organisation and individual pair? The fifth explores the existence and application of ethical codes. Finally, the sixth covers programme administration and how well participants are supported beyond the initial training and matching.

The *International Standards* are supported by experienced mentoring programme designers who have qualified as assessors. In organisations with large numbers of mentoring programmes, in-house HR professionals can train to be assessors of schemes they do not personally manage. All assessments are reviewed and monitored by a second assessor, to assure consistent quality.

A sample section of the *International Standards* is given on the next page.

STAKEHOLDER TRAINING AND BRIEFING

Participants and stakeholders understand the concept of mentoring and their respective roles.
Participants are aware of the skills and behaviours they need to apply in their roles as mentors and mentees, and have an opportunity to identify skills gaps.
Learning support is available throughout the first 12 months of their involvement in the programme.

Performance criteria	Questions	Suggested evidence
2.1 Participation in a process to learn the basics of mentoring is a non-negotiable condition of taking part in the mentoring programme, for both mentors and mentees	Is there a policy to require all mentors and mentees to attend training? Is this policy rigorously enforced (ie are there some matches made with participants who have not been trained)?	There is a record of at least some time spent learning about mentoring and associated skills by all participants. Documentation, co-ordinator interviews, participant verification
2.2 There is a clear and well-founded conceptual framework to explain mentoring functions and behaviours	Does the training material use and explain a behavioural model? Does it relate mentoring activity to a broader developmental context? Is the level of explanation appropriate for the audience? Do participants understand the model? Are they able to use it as a practical baseline for their role as mentor or mentee?	Training workbook/ materials include appropriate models. Documentation, co-ordinator interviews, participant verification
2.3 Participants obtain a clear distinction between mentoring and other forms of help and learning (eg coaching, counselling, tutoring)	Does the training material provide succinct and easily grasped distinctions? Do participants have an opportunity to discuss and internalise those distinctions? Are the boundaries between the different forms of 'helping to learn' clear? Are the commonalities between the different forms of 'helping to learn' clear?	Training workbook/ materials clarify the distinction. Documentation, co-ordinator interviews, participant verification

| 2.4 There is a clear and well-founded framework of competencies for mentors and mentees, upon which the training is based | Is there a competency base at all? Is it a proper framework, or simply a list of skills? Is it supported by research? Is it clear why these skills/ competencies are important for a mentor? Do participants have an opportunity to discuss these? | Training workbook/ materials explain competencies. Opportunity to discuss competencies. Documentation, co-ordinator interviews, participant verification |

HOW TO GET THE BEST OUT OF MENTORING PROGRAMME STANDARDS

Because they are distilled from the experiences of many organisations, with many types of scheme and in many cultures, any set of standards tends to be generic in tone. That is something of a two-edged sword. On the one hand, you know that the issues identified have proved to be significant for many other organisations, and are therefore likely to be important for your scheme too. On the other hand, you may have very specific contextual elements to compare which will not be covered by the standards.

For example, if you are managing a reverse mentoring scheme (where one party is substantially more junior in the formal hierarchy than the other, but where both take the role of mentor), then it would be helpful to be able to benchmark against other organisations with similar programmes.

The ideal situation appears to be one that integrates the formal assessment of a programme through the standards with informal benchmarking on a scheme-by-scheme basis. The European Mentoring and Coaching Council – website www.emccouncil.org.uk – is a good starting-point for finding other organisations with which to exchange data, and there is also a register of mentoring schemes on www.clutterbuckassociates.co.uk and www.coachingnet-works.org.uk. The National Mentoring Network – www.nmn.org.uk – is also able to put scheme co-ordinators in touch with other peers, primarily in schools and community programmes.

In deciding whether a set of standards will be useful for a particular scheme, it is important to consider what sort of schemes formed the core of the research. Were they mainly from one sector, or were they a few similar types of scheme?

In general, the more generic a set of standards claims to be, the vaguer the benchmarks within it. At the moment this is a moot point, as there is not much choice in standards. However, in due course it can be expected that more specific standards – say, for schemes supporting diversity objectives in the workplace – will develop out of (or in competition with) the existing standards. When this happens, making the choice between generic and specific will become an important decision in the design of the mentoring scheme.

SUMMARY

Standards will increasingly provide the benchmarks for good practice.

10

Peer and reverse mentoring

One of the primary differences between sponsorship mentoring and developmental mentoring is that the former depends on the mentor being significantly more senior in status and influence. In developmental mentoring, where what matters is the experience gap, there is a lot more room for different patterns of relationship.

Whenever any two people come together in a learning relationship, they bring a whole spectrum of different experiences, some of which may be valuable to the other person. Even in a traditional mentoring relationship, where one person is older and more senior than the other, as long as the mentor is open to learning from the more junior person, there is always substantial opportunity for exchange of knowledge, skills and insight. At the very simplest level, most of my learning about making better use of my personal computer has been gained through the patience of younger people, who have grown up in an IT environment, pointing out what is obvious to them but not to me. The exchange for them is typically induction into the wider horizons of managerial and strategic thinking.

Abandoning status and authority within a relationship not only makes for greater rapport and openness, it also influences in a very positive way the quality of learning dialogue. When one party is felt to be in some sense superior, the sense of mutual exploration and discovery is muted. To some extent this happens in all successful mentoring relationships, both developmental and sponsorship-oriented, as barriers break down. In this chapter, however, we focus on mentoring relationships that are deliberately status-free: peer mentoring and reverse mentoring.

PEER MENTORING

Mentoring between peers, although by no means as widespread in formal structures as traditional mentoring, is increasingly common. For example, newly appointed chairpersons of National Health Trusts – highly experienced, very effective people within other roles – now have the opportunity for a peer mentor while they get used to the job. In this case, there is a very specific experience gap to address. In many other examples of peer mentoring, however, particularly where the relationship is established informally, there is no single experience gap to focus upon. Both parties have simply recognised the value the other person can provide in offering support, counsel and a different perspective on the issues they face. This kind of highly accepting, let's-work-on-what-matters-at-the-moment relationship usually involves a strong sense of friendship and may have very ill-defined goals.

I have been lucky enough to have a handful of peer mentoring relationships over the years and have found that the level of challenge I receive, from someone who knows me and cares enough about me to be a critical friend, is higher than in any of the hierarchical mentoring relationships I have experienced. No one has ever been as tough on me as my peer mentors, and I am grateful for it. Beattie and McDougall (1995), who studied peer mentoring relationships at Glasgow Caledonian University, also found that trust and insight can be heightened when the participants are equal in status.

For an organisation wishing to encourage mentoring, it seems that the best way to promote informal peer mentoring is to develop the habit of mentoring through more traditional programmes. The traditional mentor can also help learners think about and develop their learning net – the web of people around them, from whom they can usefully learn. The learning net includes direct reports, people in relevant professional associations and, of course, peers either within their working area or outside.

In seeking a peer mentor, the following guidelines may be helpful:

- Look for sufficient difference in experience and personality to provide a different set of perspectives.

- Seek someone who will be genuine and honest with you, no matter how painful what they have to say may be.

- Be accessible to each other on a regular basis (e-mail makes this much easier than used to be the case – see Chapter 16).

- Try to articulate what you value in each other – this will encourage you both to approach the other whenever you have something to chew over.

- Do not regard it as an exclusive relationship; seek to develop a number of relationships with people whose perspective you value for different things.

REVERSE MENTORING

Sometimes called mutual mentoring or upward mentoring, reverse mentoring has been used successfully in a variety of companies, including GE, Procter & Gamble, BT, BP and Accenture. It differs from peer mentoring in that the partners in the relationship are from different levels in the hierarchy – sometimes several levels apart – and from traditional mentoring in that it is the hierarchically more junior person who takes the primary mentoring role, although learning is still two-way.

The stimulus for upward mentoring has arisen from two main areas of concern. In diversity programmes, one of the limiting factors on progress of women and people from minority ethnic backgrounds has been the inability of top management to understand their issues. Even though they may have attended diversity awareness workshops, emotional commitment often only comes from seeing the issues through the eyes of someone who experiences them on a frequent basis.

The second area of concern has been the recognition that senior managers are often heavily out of touch with key areas such as new technology or customer concerns. That knowledge is usually held by people at relatively junior levels. Reverse mentoring provides a mechanism to bypass the normal communication channels, which tend to sanitise knowledge, and keep the executives informed about developments they may not normally be aware of.

In essence, reverse mentoring is therefore an opportunity for a reality check at the top of the organisation. The more junior (usually younger) employees have an opportunity to observe and learn from management thinking, to influence organisational policy and to become more at ease dealing with people of substantially greater hierarchical authority.

The benefits from reversing the mentoring roles are summarised in Table 7.

Table 7 | **The benefits of reverse mentoring**

Benefits to the senior manager	Benefits to the more junior partner	Benefits to the organisation
Understanding perspectives of other groups in the organisation – gender, age, culture A sounding-board on how new policies and/or strategies may be viewed from below *Guidance on new and emerging technology* 'Friends in low places' A source of challenge to one's thinking	Visibility Access to senior management thinking A role model for own development Challenge to one's thinking Greater comfort in speaking with people in authority	Increased understanding and support for diversity management Enhanced leadership credibility Knowledge management Improved communication between layers in the organisation Constructive challenge to company policy and practice

In practice, as with the case of BP below, reverse mentoring programmes tend to avoid the issue of who is mentor and who is mentee, preferring to concentrate on the mutual learning roles. However, the very strong emphasis on the learning goals of the executives indicates where the primary intention of the relationships lies.

Reverse mentoring is becoming more common, and companies are reporting significant benefits. A number of patterns are emerging.

In some cases the relationship follows the traditional mentoring pattern – face-to-face meetings, reflective approach – but with the junior person as mentor. One government department has used its fast-track entrants to mentor senior Civil Servants. The junior mentors received training in their roles, whereas preparation of the senior mentees was done on a one-to-one basis to establish development objectives for the relationship. Great care was taken in the matching process and in follow-up support.

Several companies are using the junior mentor more directly, involving them in meetings and activities where they can observe their partner and provide direct feedback on their performance.

One programme began through a more traditional route by offering shadowing opportunities to their high-potential staff. This developed into a shadow-mentoring programme where the shadowing opportunities were balanced with time to reflect with the senior partner in a mentoring relationship. However, participants began to find benefit in providing feedback in both directions.

Non-traditional mentoring relationships flourish where thought is given to the roles of each partner. Who is the 'primary' learner? In most mentoring relationships both partners benefit, but for the mentor this is generally secondary learning and the focus is on the mentee. Will this still be the case? Because the mentor is now more junior there is often an assumption that there will continue to be direct learning for them from shared experience. All models are possible, but in setting up their relationship the pair need to be able to agree.

Being the 'mentor' in a reverse mentoring relationship is not easy. In most cases, the more junior person will have little experience at leading a learning dialogue with someone so senior. An important part of the training process, therefore is to provide skills and some frameworks to structure discussions until they flow more easily.

Where the junior mentor is giving feedback on a real-time situation, we have found that a three-stage framework helps.

- Initially, a briefing dialogue enables the pair to look at the upcoming activity and agree the focus for feedback.

- A feedback dialogue allows for full exploration of the experience.

- A debrief dialogue looks at how the mentoring process worked and how it could be improved for future sessions.

The framework puts the junior mentor comfortably into the questioning role, allowing him or her to take the lead.

Mentors, too, need time to think through the relationship so that they accept and enjoy this reversal of roles. Although supportive of the concept, it is all too easy in the mentoring meeting to slip back into default mode and for the senior person to take the lead. Having a discussion framework that is understood by both parties gives the senior person confidence in the process, allowing him or her to participate freely and both to feel less threatened.

The case studies below illustrate the kind of approaches to reverse mentoring adopted by three organisations. The Procter & Gamble case is particularly interesting because it occurs in a traditional sponsoring mentoring environment in which hierarchy and status might have been expected to create a barrier to the learning relationship. The interest in peer and reverse mentoring is growing rapidly and these approaches are likely to become increasingly significant in the design of broad mentoring capability within large organisations.

Case studies

CASE STUDY

The Cabinet Office

This case was first published in *Mentoring in Action* (Clutterbuck and Megginson, 1999). Leslie Martinson was at the time a Civil Servant in the Cabinet Office, with a role that demanded she obtain a good instinctive understanding of the world of training. Because this was not her core background, Leslie enrolled on a two-year advanced diploma programme for trainers, which encouraged participants to seek mentors. The mentor she chose was someone younger and in a grade below, but with very extensive training experience. Ignoring the status difference made for relaxed, often humorous but intense meetings, where Leslie was able to explore her progress towards becoming an effective trainer, plus a number of other personal development goals she had set for herself. The relationship survived changes of jobs on both sides, including one that took Leslie into the position of supervising her mentor's boss. The relationship dissolved as she completed the programme and both of them moved on to new fields.

CASE STUDY

Procter & Gamble

A higher turnover among women in junior and middle management posts was one of the key triggers for the Mentoring Up programme introduced in P&G's marketing division a while ago. The traditional response to this kind of problem in mentoring terms is to institute a glass ceiling programme, under which senior executives (usually predominantly male) would adopt younger, more junior protégés and nurture their progress. In this case, however, the company was astute enough to recognise that this approach (which was considered) would simply reinforce the cultural aspects of the problem. These could only be addressed by creating an environment in which the male executives learned to understand the problems of diversity for themselves. The programme that resulted provided male managers with female mentors, usually more junior than themselves, whose role was to:

- provide them with informal, non-threatening feedback on how to manage issues specific to women

- act as a sounding-board.

At the same time, the programme allowed the women mentors to develop quality relationships with people at senior level and hence to become more visible within the organisation.

The results of the initiative include a remarkable improvement in the female staff retention problem.

CASE STUDY

BP's Mutual Mentoring scheme

In 2001 BP piloted a unique upward diversity mentoring programme over eight months. Under the title of the 'Mutual Mentoring' scheme, it linked 24 individuals in the organisation to others with whom they would not normally have interacted, enabling shared learning and new insights gained from the diverse positions that each individual held.

In the BP programme, early-career professionals act as mentors to senior leaders of the company. The pairings combine genders and cultural heritages, so that junior women mentor senior men, and there are pairs of different nationalities where possible. The mentoring pairs openly discuss issues such as diversity in their mentoring meetings, and senior managers are able to gain extensive insight into race, gender, age and culture issues to which they otherwise would not be exposed.

The Mutual Mentoring scheme has made an impact on the organisation through increased awareness of gender differences and better understanding of expectations at different levels and generations. It has also stimulated creativity and innovation within BP, as well as a better awareness of diversity and inclusion concepts. Such success in the UK has helped the scheme to expand to the USA and Europe – to highly positive reviews.

SUMMARY

Peer and reverse mentoring are becoming an increasing proportion of mentoring programmes. They have a high potential to improve an organisation's use of all its talent.

11

Phases of the mentoring relationship

In an experiment with several hundred HR professionals a few years ago, I asked people who they found to be their most frequent and most intensive sources of learning at work. The results, which have since been replicated with other groups of employees in a variety of circumstances, were stark – the most frequent learning came from peers, the most intensive from mentors. Line managers scored near the bottom of the pile on both criteria.

In the traditional view of mentoring, the relationship with the mentor influences the career and personal development of a young employee. In the early stages of his or her career the young employee's identity, career aspirations and business relationships are forming. The junior must learn new technical, political and interpersonal skills. Throughout this process, the mentor relationship is often the most important vehicle for stimulating and assisting his or her development. The mentor:

- offers friendship
- acts as a role model
- accepts and confirms the mentee's notions about his or her own identity
- provides support and encouragement
- gives confidence and a feeling of competence.

The mentor also finds that a relationship with a younger employee answers certain of his or her own psychological needs. The mid-career stage can be difficult for many managers and executives as they find there is little chance of any further growth or advancement. The mentor's career may be in danger of stagnation if he or she feels locked into a pattern of repetition and uniformity. Entering a mentoring relationship at that stage of the mentor's career provides refreshing new challenges.

Mentors can redirect their energies into a stimulating and creative role. Mentoring demands a flexible and individual approach rather than applying habitual, well-used formulae. As a result, the mentor finds new self-respect as he or she recognises he or she has valuable experiences and knowledge to pass on to the mentee.

This is not necessarily the case with mentoring for people in other circumstances. For example, an executive mentee is less interested in an external mentor's knowledge of the business or the sector than in the ability to help the mentee structure and explore issues for himself or herself.

For the moment, however, let's stick with the traditional model. This is based upon a major study into the nature of the mentoring process, conducted in the early 1980s by Katherine Kram (1983), then Assistant Professor of Organisational Behaviour at Boston University's School of Management. Kram attempted to discover the significance of the relationship for the mentor and the mentee, and how mentoring influenced each party's career and self-development. She also tried to establish whether mentoring relationships share any similar characteristics.

Kram conducted her survey in a public utility company of 15,000 employees in the north-east region of the USA. She studied 18 mentoring pairs using in-depth interviews. The young mentees' ages ranged between 26 and 34, while the mentors' ages ranged between 39 and 63. The relationships varied considerably in duration, but Kram found that they were on average about five years long. Each relationship generally progressed through four distinct stages.

In the remainder of this chapter we explore each of those phases – initiation (the start), the middle period, dissolving the relationship, and restarting – alongside the slightly different evolution observed in developmental mentoring. Figure 13 outlines these differences.

Figure 13 | **The phases of relationship development: a comparison of US and European approaches**

Kram: US sponsoring mentoring		European (developmental) mentoring
Starting: Suspicion evolves into trust and mutual respect		Rapport-building, getting to know each other Direction-setting – developing a sense of relationship purpose
	6 months	
	12 months	
Middle period: Mentor uses influence to help mentee advance		Progress-making, high mutual learning
	24 months	
Working towards setting personal and career goals		Winding down: celebrating success, moving on to new sources of learning
	30 months	
Dissolving the relationship	36 months	Continuing informally, infrequently as a sounding-board
	Indeterminate	
Restarting the relationship Coming to terms with a different status		

Kram's study was based on sponsorship mentoring and a definition that included both off-line and boss-subordinate relationships, so its general applicability to developmental mentoring is suspect. The phases she identifies ring broadly true, however, even if the conclusions drawn are not the same.

THE START OF THE RELATIONSHIP

During the first six months to a year of a successful mentoring relationship, says Kram, the young mentee may well hold an unrealistically ideal picture of the mentor. He or she frequently sees the mentor as an extremely competent figure who gives support and guidance. In these circumstances the mentee identifies strongly with the mentor and draws emotional support from the relationship. The young manager feels that he or she is cared for by someone of great importance within the organisation. The opposite, of course, may also occasionally be the case. A mentee may begin the relationship with a great deal of suspicion and an image of the more senior manager as a 'played-out timeserver'. How well the mentoring relationship works here will depend on whether the mentor wins the mentee's respect as the nature of the job he or she does and the difficulty of the decisions he or she takes become clearer.

For the mentor, the relationship with the mentee can also be highly rewarding during this period. The mentor is drawn to the mentee because of his or her potential and willingness to learn, seeing in the mentee someone to whom his or her own values and perspectives can be passed. In a successful relationship, mentors also derive satisfaction from recognising how they can speed the mentee's growth by supplying advice and support. Many mentors also comment on the sense of pride they have in seeing their mentees progress. Both mentor and mentee develop positive expectations of each other. By the end of the first year they have gained sufficient confidence in each other and in the relationship to set in motion more substantial arrangements for learning.

Observation of European mentoring relationships presents a somewhat different picture. For a start, the initiation phase seems to have two components – rapport-building and direction-setting. During rapport-building, the mentor and mentee test the water – can they work together easily? Deep friendship is not required, simply sufficient mutual respect, goodwill and relevance of experience to begin the journey. Learning how to work together is a process of sharing that will gradually increase in intimacy as trust grows and positive experience of achieving useful insights accumulates. The mentor needs to exercise considerable skill at putting the mentee at ease, encouraging him or her to open up.

Direction-setting involves developing a consensus about the outcomes the mentee desires and some practical ideas about how to get there. The mentor needs considerable skills in helping the mentee clarify personal goals, build commitment to them and develop a practical and, if appropriate, opportunistic plan to achieve the relationship goals. The mentor may also be quite open about his or her own learning goals from the relationship – which in turn helps to reinforce the building of rapport.

A checklist for the first meeting

1   Where shall we meet, and for how long?

    PROP (Professional, Relaxed, Open, Purposeful) for both parties

2   What do we want/need to know about each other?

    Social:

- career history
- domestic circumstances
- interests outside work

    Career ambition:

- what you enjoy/dislike about working in this industry
- where you want to be in five years' time
- greatest achievements/failures
- what your picture of success is
- how clear the mentee's career goals are

    Development goals:

- what the mentee wants to improve in for the current job
- in preparation for future jobs
- where the mentee would most value guidance/advice/a sounding-board

3   What will make this a satisfying and useful relationship for both of us?

4   What expectations do we have of each other (ground rules and verbal contract)?

5   What are our priorities?

6   How often and where shall we meet?

7   Do we want to set an agenda for our next meeting?

8   Are there any issues we should get to work on now?

THE MIDDLE PERIOD

Kram's middle period lasts for two to five years and is regarded as the most rewarding for the two parties. The relationship is cultivated as the mentor coaches and promotes his or her mentee. The friendship between the two strengthens as a high degree of trust and intimacy builds up between the mentor and mentee.

The mentor's ability to coach the mentee and clarify his or her sense of purpose and identity helps to improve the mentee's sense of self-worth. In sponsoring mentoring, the mentor provides the mentee with work opportunities that help to develop his or her managerial skills and confirm and reinforce the mentee's sense of competence and ability. The mentee understands the business scenario better and knows how better to control the work environment.

One mentee commented:

> *I was very under-confident when I joined this company. I was newly divorced and I had not worked for quite some time. I was wholly intimidated by the business world. My mentor encouraged me to perform beyond my job description. She would criticise my performance, explain my mistakes and advise me on how to perform better. Above all, she gave me confidence. She would say 'I know that you have the ability to do it, and I know that you will do it.' Her encouragement and faith in me was a great support and incentive.*

It is at this stage that the mentor gains the most satisfaction from the knowledge that he or she has had an important effect on the mentee's development. One mentor tries to describe the pride he feels when he sees his mentee perform well and receive recognition from the company:

> *The satisfaction I receive is similar to parental pride. You have put faith in that person and helped them develop. When they succeed, you feel it has all been worthwhile and you remember that you were instrumental in helping them to do so.*

Mentors also receive technical and psychological help and support from their mentees. The mentee now has the skill to help his or her mentor as well as the ability to recognise the needs of the more senior manager. The mentor has a renewed sense of his or her own influence and power as he or she opens doors in the organisation for the mentee. The mentor also feels that he or she is passing something to the company that will have lasting value. Through the mentee the sponsoring mentor can express his or her own perspectives and values.

In Kram's scenario, it often takes until this point for the mentor and the mentee to have agreed upon a set of development goals or even a career path, involving at least one and usually several clearly defined promotional or horizontal moves. Discussions between the mentor and mentee now centre less on defining objectives than on strategies and tactics to achieve them. Project work that the line manager mentor sets his or her mentee is aimed both at developing skills and at assessing how well they have been absorbed. The two people meet regularly to review progress in each area where they have agreed improvement is necessary to qualify for the next career step. The mentor directs the mentee towards additional sources of learning and challenges him or her to prove the successes claimed.

Again the picture that emerges from developmental mentoring is different in a number of ways. For a start, the time horizon is often much shorter – many developmental mentoring relationships are well into the middle (or the progress-making) period after six months or so. Second, the mentor has no role in the projects or tasks the mentee undertakes, other than as a sounding-board. Third, the developmental mentoring relationship at this stage is characterised by a much deeper level of challenge, probing and analysis. Fourth, the mentee begins to rely much more on his or her own judgement, and is less likely to seek the mentor's approval.

Finally, the mentor often learns as much or more from their dialogue as does the mentee. This highly fulfilling phase of the relationship often settles down to a routine in which the pair are sufficiently familiar and comfortable with the process to explore more and more 'difficult' issues. Sensitive areas that the mentee has avoided now become admissible and may provide the deepest and most transforming issues for discussion.

Throughout this whole progress-making phase, the effective mentor demonstrates a remarkably consistent skill set – consistent, that is, with every other effective mentor. Figure 14 is based on observation of numerous mentors, ranging from the very effective to the very ineffective.

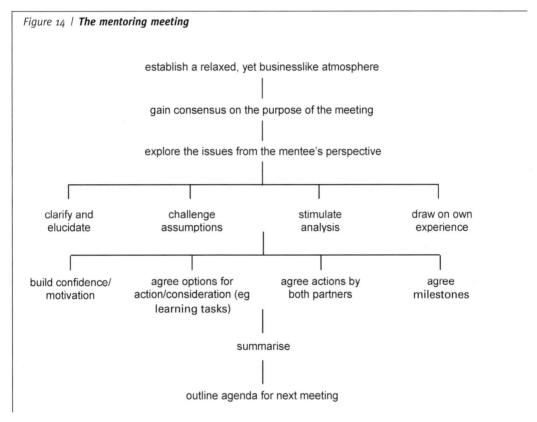

Figure 14 | **The mentoring meeting**

establish a relaxed, yet businesslike atmosphere

gain consensus on the purpose of the meeting

explore the issues from the mentee's perspective

| clarify and elucidate | challenge assumptions | stimulate analysis | draw on own experience |

| build confidence/ motivation | agree options for action/consideration (eg learning tasks) | agree actions by both partners | agree milestones |

summarise

outline agenda for next meeting

The most effective mentors, even those who are strongly activist and/or task-oriented, always start the process by re-establishing rapport. For a few minutes they engage in the normal social trivialities that help people relax in each other's company. Then they ask the mentee to explain briefly what issues he or she would like to explore. One of my favourite questions to executive mentees is, 'What's keeping you awake at night this week?'

Ineffective mentors listen briefly to the mentee's account and immediately relate the issue to their own experience, when they perceive it to be relevant. They tell the mentee what happened to them, how they tackled the issue, and what lessons they learned. As a result, they frequently end up advising on the presented issue, missing deeper, more important issues. Effective mentors hold fire. First, they ask for more facts and feelings – what exactly happened? How did you feel about it? Is this a one-off occurrence?

Next, they challenge the assumptions behind the mentee's account – for example, what would an unbiased third party have thought if they were observing? The responses to this probing, and the different perspectives generated, allow mentor and mentee to analyse the situation in some form of conceptual framework. For example, 'Let's look at how your behaviour might be influencing your colleagues, and vice versa.'

Finally, in this first half of the mentoring session, the mentor may draw upon his or her own experience to introduce additional considerations.

Having understood the issues better, mentor and mentee can concentrate on developing pragmatic solutions. Before launching into problem-solving mode, however, the mentor ensures that the mentee is in a sufficiently positive frame of mind – that he or she has the confidence to consider alternative approaches and the commitment to making a change happen. Through a variety of techniques, the mentor helps the mentee catalogue possible ways forward and assess them against the mentee's own values criteria. Having selected one or two to pursue, the pair agree who will do what in dealing with the issue. Ineffective mentors sometimes tend to take on extensive responsibilities; effective ones limit their role to tasks such as seeking out an article or report, or making an introduction. The effective mentor also presses the mentee to set mental deadlines by which he or she expects to have tackled at least the initial stages of the plan.

One final task remains – summarising what has been discussed. Ineffective mentors rush straight in and summarise for the mentee. In doing so, they both miss the chance to check that there is a common understanding and take responsibility for the issue at least partly back on to their own shoulders. Effective mentors ensure that the mentee summarises and retains ownership of the issue throughout, including whether to bring the matter back to the agenda next time they meet.

DISSOLVING THE RELATIONSHIP

In Kram's model, after two to five years the mentoring relationship begins to draw apart. The mentor and the mentee are affected by organisational changes. The mentee has advanced sufficiently to be experiencing new independence and autonomy. The mentor relationship becomes less essential as the mentee's challenges change.

Mentees may respond differently when the relationship declines, according to how prepared they are for the separation. If a change in career position occurs before the mentee feels ready to operate independently of the mentor, he or she will experience a time of uncertainty and anxiety. The mentee will miss the psychological support of the mentor and be aware that he or she no longer has a 'safety net' to fall upon if he or she makes a wrong decision. The unprepared mentee can also feel abandoned and betrayed and lose confidence.

One young British mentee found her first year apart from her mentor a very difficult time emotionally. A period of redefinition was necessary as she had to demonstrate to the rest of the organisation that she was able to operate independently without her mentor:

> *I had to prove to myself and the rest of the company that it was my ability which got me my new job and not my mentor's influence. I had to show I could stand alone. I think the whole process helped me to mature. Now if I have any difficulties I rely on myself.*

If the mentee is fully prepared for separation from the mentor, he or she enjoys this new-found freedom and independence. It is a little like driving the car home after having passed the driving test. Most mentors accept that their mentees must move away from them and become psychologically more self-sufficient.

Even after the separation has taken place, the mentor continues to encourage the mentee to move forward in his or her career. In sponsorship mentoring, the mentor will often promote the mentee at a distance and be kept informed of the mentee's progress. However, some mentors are unwilling to allow their mentees to go beyond their influence and control. This is most common in senior executives who are insecure in their own positions. The mentor tends to project his or her own negative career expectations on to the mentee. If the mentor feels he or she can go no higher in the company, he or she is likely to feel that a subordinate will not either.

Some managers whose own careers have stagnated and offer little hope for future advancement resent a mentee who has more career opportunities. This kind of mentor does not want the mentee to outstrip him or her, and as a result attempts to delay the mentee's movement by insisting that the mentee stay in the same position.

Where the mentee feels ready to break the mentoring relationship but is unable to move beyond the mentor's sphere of influence, he or she may feel frustrated, restless and ultimately hostile. This is another argument against the use of the immediate boss as a mentor. Although such feelings can be absorbed across departmental boundaries, they may be explosive within the department. Some companies use the personnel department, the mentoring co-ordinator or an arbitrator in senior management to ensure that the mentee has someone to appeal to if conflict of this kind arises. (The mentor, too, can use this formal route to express disquiet if he or she believes a mentee is being pushed too fast for his or her own good.) Such arbitration is rare, however, not least because the numbers of people involved in most companies are sufficiently small for the issues to be resolved by informal means.

For both the mentor and the mentee the period of divorce and separation is important for their reputation and career in the organisation. The mentee demonstrates his or her skills and independence while the mentor shows to colleagues and other potential mentees that he or she develops young people successfully. The progress of the mentee proves the accuracy of the mentor's insight into potential. By now, the mentee's career objectives may have changed several times as the mentor has made him or her aware of new opportunities and expected changes in the organisation. The mentee will have gradually assumed more and more of the responsibility for his or her own career objectives and will increasingly be taking the initiative in seeking out training opportunities and experience that will help him or her achieve his or her goals. In effect, the mentor has taught what he or she knows and there is little more to pass on.

In developmental mentoring the dynamic is subtly different, not least because it is extremely rare for this kind of dependency to develop in the first place. In a relationship where the primary purpose is achieving rapid self-reliance and where the mentor is not expected to use his or her power on behalf of the mentee, winding down is a relatively straightforward affair. In many cases where a formal time limit has been built into the scheme from the start, both parties begin to prepare for dissolution long before it begins. (In a mentoring scheme run by Shell, it was noticeable that in the relationships with the least time to run – because the mentor would be repatriated in 12–18 months – the intensity of the relationship and the learning was higher than in those where the time-frame was more relaxed. The mentees knew they had to get every drop of learning they could while they could.)

At least one meeting before the expected formal end of the relationship, mentor and mentee should begin to review:

- what the relationship has delivered in terms of expected and unexpected outcomes (changes in knowledge, behaviour, role, etc) for both parties

- what it has *not* delivered

- what they expect for the new (informal) phase of the relationship, if there is to be one

- what future mentoring needs the mentee may have that may best be met by other people.

In a recent study of relationship endings, David Megginson and I (2003) compared the experiences of numerous mentors and mentees. They fell into two clear categories:

- those whose formal relationship had a clear ending, in which they reviewed (and in some cases celebrated) what they had achieved together – these were almost all perceived as positive by both mentor and mentee

- those whose relationship had just drifted away over time, and which were almost always seen as negative.

Mentors and mentees whose relationship had wound down – rather than wound up – tended to feel unsure about their contribution, and sometimes betrayed. By contrast, recognising the value of the relationship enabled both parties to move on with confidence.

RESTARTING THE RELATIONSHIP

In Kram's analysis both mentee and mentor continue to have some form of interaction, although it is on a more casual basis. The relationship enters a new stage where the mentee and mentor regard each other as equals. The relationship now develops into a friendship, the two maintaining contact with each other on the basis of mutual advantage rather than upon the primarily one-sided career advantage once offered. The mentee ceases to identify with the mentor, whose weaknesses he or she now recognises alongside the strengths that had seemed so impressive in the early stages of the relationship. The bond of gratitude takes over from the bond of need. When the two become peers in the organisation, uncertainty and discomfort may occur as they adjust to the new role relationship.

This new transition can also be characterised by hostility and resentment between the mentee and the mentor. The mentee may have found it difficult to make a complete break from the mentor. When the two meet again on a more equal footing, the mentee often feels that he or she will fall into the former dependent role. To prevent this, the mentee behaves aggressively to the mentor and the former intimacy is not re-established.

In developmental mentoring, a similar but gentler transition occurs. Mentor and mentee often continue to meet, but now informally, with no organisational support, no agenda, and much lower frequency. When they do meet, it is as equals, whatever their relative status in the organisation – each sees the other as a useful sounding-board, a learning resource and a valuable person in their networks. Meetings will be much more spontaneous and relaxed, less focused, often based upon the fact that they both happen to be in the same place at the same time.

SUMMARY

Clearly, every mentoring relationship is unique, just as every individual is unique. But a high proportion of relationships do seem to follow either the Kram stages of development if it is a sponsoring mentoring scheme, or the European four-phase model if it is a developmental scheme. In either case, to minimise the problems and maximise the benefits of mentoring both the mentor and the mentee must be well briefed on how the relationship may develop. The company, too, needs to monitor the stages of development to provide the external support that will head off serious problems before they occur.

12

Problems of mentoring programmes and relationships

Although mentoring is a powerful human resource development tool, it is only one of many in the corporate toolbox. Badly handled, it can turn into a spanner in the works. Even well handled, it is not appropriate in all circumstances, nor is it necessarily superior to other forms of management development. Rather, it is a process to be used alongside other, more traditional forms of career progression. Many companies that have been running mentoring programmes during the past decade now encourage managers to have as many developmental relationships of different kinds as possible.

Katherine Kram (1983) puts the negative side of a wholehearted corporate commitment to mentoring:

> *The concept has become too aggrandized. Mentoring can sometimes be limited in value or even destructive in a company.*

> *Career development staff should remember that other relationships, for example with peers, can be just as rewarding and fruitful as mentoring relationships.*

(Note the assumption that peers do not mentor each other!)

Some companies have found that the main problem is the unfamiliarity of mentoring in the business environment. Other critics say that true mentor-mentee relationships are rare and should not develop at gunpoint. Michael Zey in his book *The Mentor Connection* feels that trying to formalise 'what is at best a random occurrence' can prove disastrous if management does not stand by the newly joined couples.

Some formal mentoring is seen as a quick fix for companies who should really be looking at changing their whole culture. Reba Keele, Assistant Professor of Organisational Behaviour at Brigham Young University, Utah, feels that formal mentoring, like arranged marriages, works better in Far Eastern cultures than in Western. In Japan especially, she points out, the traditional respect for age and experience provides a framework that most people can accept:

> *In the Japanese organization, the senior member of management has already accepted the fact that he is not going to become the next president. Assuming the responsibility of mentoring is considered an honor and recognition of your status. Whereas in our organizations, issues that have to do with human resource development are not considered primary functions.*

Organisations should monitor the programme carefully so that they can identify and solve problems swiftly. Most difficulties can easily be resolved if they are recognised early and brought out into the open. Clear lines of communication between mentors, mentees and programme co-ordinators can ensure that dissatisfactions with the relationship will result in immediate action.

We can divide the most common pitfalls into those that concern the programme and those that concern the individual mentoring relationship.

ORGANISATIONAL ISSUES

Poor planning and preparation

Unclear programme objectives, failure to gain the public endorsement of senior managers, and under-resourcing the programme are all common failings.

A division of a large US-based multinational insisted that its operations around the world all instituted mentoring programmes for a particular group of employees before the year end, a mere four months away. The number of relationships established would be measured and 'heads would roll' if the policy were not implemented enthusiastically. Of course, local senior management responded on the hoof, informing several hundred people in the UK alone that they would be mentor or mentee to someone else. Because no one knew what they were doing and there had been no time to gain participants' buy-in, most of the relationships got off to a rocky start. As long as it measured only the number of assigned pairings, the US head office was happy. Only when it started to look at the frequency and quality of meetings did it realise that all but a small handful of the relationships were anything more than a sham.

Poor clarity of role

Failure to distinguish between the roles of the line manager and the mentor leads to confusion and sometimes to conflict between mentor and line manager. Expecting the mentor to take part in appraising the mentee can also be confusing, on both sides, and lead the mentee to be very cautious about what he or she says. However, it is possible to be quite ingenious in managing this kind of potential conflict of role.

At Perot Systems, where most employees work in multiple teams, there is often no single stable point of supervision to carry out an appraisal. Instead, the individual's mentor – or in some cases, the individual – gathers appraisal feedback from a mixture of the mentee's peers, project team leaders and internal customers. This information becomes neutral information – not the mentor's opinion – which the mentor helps the mentee deal with. In this way, there is no need for the mentee to 'play up' to the mentor.

Failure to set and measure clear outcomes

Many schemes get introduced because someone thinks it would be generally a good thing. So it might, but in the absence of clear expected outcomes, the scheme may easily fall into disrepute as just another talking-shop.

Although mentoring may not involve a lot of direct cost, it does require a lot of valuable management time. Top management is justified in asking for some kind of demonstrable return on the investment. Schemes that build in relevant measurement from the start arguably have a better chance of securing and retaining top management support.

Too little or too much formality

A mentoring scheme aimed at helping children from deprived backgrounds develop literacy and numeracy skills initially required every mentor and mentee to complete a six-page detailed report after each meeting. It had not occurred to the organisers that the target audience of mentees might be intimidated by all this. Getting the balance right between formality and informality is not easy. There has to be enough formality to create a supportive framework, in which relationships can flourish, but enough informality for each mentoring pair to develop its own relationship as it feels fit. Paradoxically, the better trained the mentors and mentees are, the more confident both they and the organisation can feel in allowing relationships to develop in their own way.

Failure to quality-control the mentor pool

It is now generally regarded as good practice to insist that mentoring relationships will only be sanctioned and supported by the organisation if the mentor and mentee have both attended at least a minimal level of training. Some companies use the mentor training sessions as subtle assessment centres for the mentors – people who demonstrate a complete unsuitability for the role can have their cards marked and, unless somebody specifically asks for them as a mentor, will never be drawn from the pool. These companies also take the view that anyone who volunteers as a mentor should be allowed to attend the training. First, some of the skills and techniques may rub off on them and be used in their dealings with their direct reports. Second, they may decide to become a mentee rather than a mentor. On several occasions when the latter has occurred, the person concerned has grown in the role of mentee – using his or her own mentor as a role model for his or her own attempts at acquiring better developmental skills – and eventually become an effective mentor.

Where any old manager, selected by seniority rather than developmental competence, is placed into the role, it requires a strong mentee to demand and obtain the kind of deep dialogue he or she needs. The relationship may also require a considerable input of time by the programme co-ordinator, which might be better spent elsewhere. A curious logic often operates in large corporations, however: 'We are a world-class company, employing highly intelligent, world-class people. So all of our senior managers should by definition be good at developing other people. So they should all become mentors.' If all promotions were truly made because managers were good at the people skills, this logic might – just – stand up. But the reality is that managers still primarily get promoted for task achievement and organisational ability, rather than for their skills at developing others. Once a very senior person takes on the title of mentor, there may be little appetite from the mentee, the scheme co-ordinator or anyone else to tell him or her that he or she is not doing a good job. The mentor bumbles along in blissful ignorance, the mentee feels trapped and, if there are enough people in the same situation, a deep cynicism about the whole approach establishes itself.

These managers may also help to perpetuate stereotypes both in a company's management style and in its culture. Ideas and values that senior executives pass down to mentees may in reality be obsolete or irrelevant. If these values are too vigorously imposed, junior employees are discouraged from finding their own methods and instead use old solutions for new problems. As a result, the company becomes entrenched in the past and loses its ability to react quickly to the demands of the present.

Being too elitist

Some programmes for high-flyers deliberately set out to be elitist. They want participants to recognise that being chosen as a mentee is a mark of the company's confidence in their potential. There is a downside, however – what about those left out? Since most organisations have a pyramidal structure, it follows that there will always be some junior managers who have a mentor and some who do not. There are just not enough mentors to go round, so a company faces the constant danger of alienating failed candidates.

Unfortunately, the resentment and disappointment felt by failed applicants can outweigh the benefits that successful candidates receive from the programme. A junior who does not gain entry all too often believes the selectors' decision to be based on his or her own personal limitations, rather than due to a lack of programme resources. He or she believes that it is an unspoken statement by the company indicating that he or she lacks the ability to fill important positions in the future. In short, he or she has been given a vote of no confidence.

One UK company with a number of geographically spread operations invited applications for the pilot of its mentoring programme. More than 40 people applied for the 15 available places. Although the company wrote to all the unsuccessful candidates suggesting they speak to their local employee counsellor, only one did so – and she handed in her notice. The company learned that it had to:

- make sure everyone knew the criteria for selection
- demonstrate that mentoring was just one route to advancement among many
- consider unsuccessful candidates' reactions at a much earlier stage.

Such negative experiences can be very damaging to a junior manager. His or her self-confidence and morale may be eroded to such an extent as to underrate his or her own ability and potential, and to lower his or her career aspirations accordingly. As a result, instead of having a motivated young employee who aims at promotion through a high standard of work, a company has an individual whose enthusiasm is curbed and who ceases to stretch his or her abilities because there seems to be no reward in doing so.

Alternatively, a failed candidate can feel resentment and bitterness as he or she sees peers receive treatment that seems 'preferential'. 'Favouritism' is a frequently heard complaint, as well as the accusation that peers used unfair tactics to gain a place on the programme. A mentee's friendship with a senior executive becomes 'sucking up' or 'crawling'. Envy and resentment from a mentee's peers can frequently hinder, or even destroy, a mentoring programme.

It is probably not possible to assure everyone that the selection process for high-flyer mentoring has been totally fair, and there will always be a few individuals who convince themselves that the programme caters only for those who are best at impressing the right people rather than those who are most able and deserving.

Being too problem-focused

When young graduates on the Bank of England's mentoring programme failed to meet their mentors as frequently as expected and failed to gather much value from the relationship, investigation showed that there were two main causes. One was a reluctance to disturb someone more senior, and obviously very busy, with their own relatively trivial issues. The other was a perception that mentors were there to help you deal with problems, rather than to help you identify and manage opportunities. These highly intellectually capable young men and women perceived that it was not career-enhancing behaviour to admit weaknesses to anyone else in the organisation, even within a relationship of confidentiality. Greater clarity at the beginning about how mentors could add value to their personal development and career planning might have overcome some of these problems, along perhaps with a deferment of the programme until they had been with the bank long enough to develop their own ideas about how they would use a mentor and what sort of mentor would best suit them.

Power alignments

Primarily a problem of sponsorship mentoring, the issue of power underlies a whole raft of common problems with mentoring schemes. For example, by assigning a mentor to a mentee in a different department or a different division, a company changes the nature of its informal structure. Close relationships that extend beyond the normal business restraints and that cut across the barrier of status and position mean that new alliances are formed between junior and senior employees. A company that has run a mentoring programme for several years may have the additional power nexus of a former mentor and a mentee, now on the same organisational rung, actively promoting and assisting each other. While this means the informal communications of a company are strengthened, it can also lead to an increase in corporate politics.

One of the objectives of the mentoring programme is at least partly to overcome the unfairness of the informal old boy networks. Unless the company is vigilant, there is a very real danger that instead of making the system more open and fair, the scheme may simply create new closed networks. If covert sources of information are available only to the chosen few within mentor-mentee relationships, only the initiated know how to gain and use company resources effectively. Through this, mentors and mentees can form a small yet powerful group capable of operating through and beyond the company's formal positions of power.

Before BP Chemicals began its mentoring programme, doubters thought it would interfere with the authority and skills of the line manager and would set up a network independent of management control. In practice, these fears proved groundless, to the extent that the pilot plant's managers changed from sceptics to enthusiasts.

Failure to make it clear from the outset that the young person is still primarily responsible to his or her immediate boss and not to his or her mentor can create serious power-play problems. The mentor has to guard against creating situations where the mentee uses his or her special relationship to bypass the authority of his or her boss. At the same time, the mentor must not override the mentee's boss, other than in exceptional cases. Unfortunately, obscuring the company's command structure can happen all too easily. Because the mentor and mentee are adhering to a different system of loyalty and authority, they cut across the recognised formal hierarchy. An invisible chain of command can emerge subtly to challenge the established one, resulting in confusion, conflict and bitterness.

The mentee's immediate superior can often be placed in an uncomfortable and difficult position by all this. A brittle relationship can develop between the mentee, the manager and the mentor if the manager is completely excluded from the relationship, perhaps only learning about it by accident. The manager in this situation feels threatened and frequently resents the mentor's behaviour, interpreting it as open interference. If the mentor overrides the manager's authority, the latter will feel his or her authority is being publicly undermined. Inevitably, the manager will resort to obstructing the mentoring relationship in order to protect his or her own position.

An experienced mentoring scheme administrator, quoted in a US newsletter, points out that it is only natural for the mentee's boss, who after all has a department to run, to be jealous of the mentor's influence – especially if the mentor has a powerful position in the organisation. 'Remember that the boss is the boss,' he advises would-be mentors. 'And don't let your own experiences blind you to the realities. The last thing a mentee needs is advice from the mentor that leads to conflict with the supervisor.' Had the line manager been involved in the programme from the beginning, he might have been more co-operative.

It is important that the mentor and line manager should not be seen to collude together, or even to discuss the mentee (this would make it difficult for the mentee to give full trust to the mentor). One company asks line managers to take prospective mentees to the mentor's office for the first meeting. In another, line managers and mentors are briefed together.

In companies where there are a large number of middle manager positions and few senior positions, mentors again need to conduct their mentoring relationships carefully. A manager who is unlikely to be promoted further may resent the fact that the mentee beneath him or her is being groomed for advancement. The manager will realise that he or she has been passed over by the company and could possibly attempt to hinder the mentee's prospects by writing unfavourable reports. In this situation the mentor and the mentee need to try to make the relationship between them as invisible as possible.

Some salutary examples

Company A launched its mentoring scheme with a memo to its chief executives across Europe, instructing them to ensure that the top 100 women employees in the region were given mentors. The first the mentors and mentees knew about it was when they also received a memo telling them that they were participants in the programme and who they had been paired up with. Mentors and mentees met up for lunch, in most cases with very little idea of what was expected of them and what outcomes should come from the mentoring process. Six months later, only three pairs were still meeting regularly. Lack of clarity of purpose, lack of skills in the role and a feeling of being press-ganged not only prevented most people establishing a positive learning relationship but ensured that their cynicism spread to participants in other planned programmes.

Company B decided it would 'help' mentors and mentees have meaningful discussions by insisting they meet every two weeks and giving them a detailed sheet of topics to consider. It also demanded a written record of what had been discussed, in broad terms. Mentors and mentees felt they were not trusted and struggled to establish and maintain rapport. Most relationships drowned in the bureaucracy. Those that survived subverted or ignored the rules and simply concentrated on issues of concern to the mentee at the time.

Company C went for the 'sheep-dip' approach, assuming that only mentors needed training. Because the mentors were very senior, training was limited to just two hours and was mainly about explaining the role. When the relationships failed to gel, one-to-one interviews with the senior managers revealed what they would not admit in public or to their peer group that they felt inadequate for the role because they lacked a wide enough portfolio of skills and techniques.

RELATIONSHIP ISSUES

Failure to establish rapport

In general, if two people do not 'click' within the first two meetings, the relationship is unlikely to develop the depth of trust and mutual confidence that allows mentor and mentee to address intimate issues. Having a clear developmental goal to work on (ie the mentee's learning, support or career needs) provides a significant boost to the rapport-building process – if only because it provides a clear, shared point of reference and interest. You can learn to value, like and respect someone relatively easily if you work with him or her on something that is important to you.

The reality is, however, that some relationships are not going to work. For example, a middle-aged engineer found he simply could not develop rapport with a highly assertive young woman graduate. Part of the problem, he admitted, was that he kept slipping back into behavioural routines he had developed with his daughter, who was of a similar age and temperament. These routines typically involved a lot of telling and a fair amount of shouting. This was potentially an ideal opportunity for some reverse mentoring, in which he would have learned from the graduate how to understand his daughter's perspective, but he decided to withdraw from the programme altogether.

Rapport demands that both parties share or at least acknowledge the validity of each other's values. In the absence of this consensus it is always better to dissolve the relationship and help the mentee find someone with whom he or she is more compatible.

Lack of time

All mentoring relationships suffer from time and diary pressures – in every survey of mentoring problems I have seen, time is one of the top three issues. By definition, people who have the most wisdom to pass on are likely to be among the busiest. Mentees may also be drawn from among ambitious groups of people who are themselves working long hours. Yet both mentors and mentees typically do find the time.

In general, it seems, the people who do not make the time are those who do not have the commitment and who do not get a buzz out of reflective dialogue and increasing self-knowledge. Other people find ways around the problem – for example, by developing a rolling three-meeting schedule so that a change of date one month does not lead to diary drift the next.

Sometimes what looks like a dead relationship is simply suffering from an overwhelming demand on the mentor's time. In a multinational telecom company, one of a batch of international cross-border relationships had got nowhere after four months. The mentee had chased the mentor frequently, but had only received short e-mails in reply. Then, on the day of a review session, the mentee reported enthusiastically that he had at last spent some telephone time with his mentor, who apologised profusely and explained he had been moved suddenly to take up a major post in another country. Now that he was settled in, however, he was determined to make the relationship work and would fly to Europe in a week or so specifically to hold the first formal meeting.

Clarity of relationship purpose

If mentor and mentee do not agree fairly quickly on some goals that the mentee would like to achieve and on which the mentor can help, the relationship will swiftly drive into the sand. It does not matter that the goals change over time – the sense of purpose drives the frequency of meetings and the focus on real issues.

Expecting too much of each other

For either the mentor or the mentee to bring a set of unrealistic expectations to the relationship is unlikely to be helpful. In theory, the initial discussions and psychological contract should clarify expectations at all levels. But poor mentors often fail to carry the process through. For example, according to Katherine Kram (1983), when the mentee realises the mentor is unable to transform his or her career, the mentee may feel resentful and betrayed.

Mentees must be realistic from the beginning, she says. They should not expect the relationship to meet every need, nor for it to continue indefinitely. 'Mentors provide different degrees of mentoring, and the mentee should accept this,' she maintains.

Some mentors cross a fine line too easily between exhibiting confidence in a mentee and expecting too much. One young executive was forced to leave his job because of the unbearable pressure his mentor unknowingly placed upon him. He explains:

> He seemed to think I could do anything that he asked me to do. Eventually it got to the stage where I was terrified he would discover I was not a whiz kid and was in fact quite average. My position was made so unbearable by my mentor that I decided to quit.

Had his mentor directed him towards additional training in key areas, he might well have gained the confidence to cope.

Allowing dependency to develop

Primarily an issue for sponsorship mentoring, dependency is unhealthy for both parties. Kram (1983) provides the example of a divisional manager who wished to move to headquarters and could not understand why the company was so reluctant to transfer him:

> I begged the powers that be to move me, yet they refused to alter their position. I was mystified until a colleague told me that my mentor had insisted that I was not ready for the move. The only thing I could do was to make it clear to him that I was grateful for all the help he had given my career, yet nevertheless I was determined to move on – or move out. He denied any involvement, but a month later I was transferred. The evidence seemed to speak for itself.

Problems with other people

The literature on mentoring contains a variety of references to problems with spouses, line managers and working colleagues. Most of these can be avoided by being very open about the relationship.

Problems with spouses tend to be most common with mixed-gender mentoring relationships, for obvious reasons. These relationships can also generate malicious gossip. Experienced mentors avoid these problems by having a number of mentees of both sexes and by holding meetings relatively publicly.

Problems with line managers occur most often when the line manager feels threatened. Is the mentee badmouthing him or her to someone more senior? Is the mentor – perhaps from the best of motives – using his or her position of greater seniority to give the mentee developmental tasks that prevent the mentee from spending essential time on line responsibilities? The potential for conflict is substantial, yet most organisations avoid it.

Some, such as BP Chemicals, involve the line manager to the extent of taking the mentee to meet the mentor for the first time. Others ensure that mentors and line managers are fully briefed about their respective roles.

A lot of problems with other employees can be overcome by providing clear briefings about the nature of mentoring and how it fits into the portfolio of development opportunities. A pilot programme should always be marketed as such, with a clear statement that if it is successful, it will be rolled out to as many other groups as possible. (That gives everyone who is envious a reason to help make the scheme work!)

SUMMARY

Mentoring should not be the only form of career or personal development within the organisation. The company must also be aware of the problems and the conflicts that the mentoring pair may experience with the mentee's boss and peers. Careful selection and preparation of both mentor and mentee can avoid both these problems and others that may arise with the mentoring relationship itself.

Part 4:

Specific mentoring issues

13

Graduate mentoring

TEN KEYS FOR THE SUCCESSFUL GRADUATE MENTORING SCHEME

The transition from education to the world of work can come as a bit of a shock. The nature of learning – and the speed with which it has to take place – is considerably different. Instead of pursuing a self-focused goal (getting a degree), the graduate is expected to share team learning and team goals. Different behaviours, different thinking patterns, the need to develop some clarity of personal purpose and direction, the need to build effective networks of influence and information – these are all classic situations addressed by mentoring.

It is no coincidence, then, that formal mentoring schemes in the UK and Europe were almost all aimed at graduates until the mid-1990s. Companies could see immediate advantages in attracting and keeping this valuable asset. Pilkington, among others, calculated the cost savings to the company of having graduates stay longer and contribute sooner. One large packaging company found that its graduates, teamed with mentors to address long-standing but low-priority technical problems in production, saved more through quality improvements than the entire training and recruitment budget for all staff on site!

It did not always work out so well, however. Many schemes either collapsed as pressures of change made it more difficult for mentors to provide quality time, or simply faded away because there was no real ownership. A new phase of graduate mentoring can now be discerned in many organisations – one that is characterised by greater realism and a stronger determination to make graduate mentoring part of the organisational infrastructure.

A lot of lessons have been learned. The following represent a mixture of the most common and the most important.

1 Managing the power distance

Early graduate mentoring schemes adopted an American model and matched young people with very senior people – often at or just below the board. They were almost universally wasted. The executives could not empathise with the situation of someone just starting out on their career. They either preached at the graduates or tried to relive their own careers through them. They had neither the time nor the inclination to act as anything but sponsors (a small part of the potential role and now generally discouraged in European mentoring schemes), and they learned little in return.

Good practice now is to limit the size of the hierarchy and experience gaps, to promote empathy and mutual learning. The trick is to have enough scope for the graduate to respect and value the mentor's experience, but to be close enough to develop a genuine rapport.

2 Timing the start of the relationship

Most schemes even now assume that the mentoring relationship should begin as soon as the graduate arrives. Practical experience increasingly brings that assumption into question. It seems that a significant minority of relationships fail to gel because the graduate simply does not know enough about the organisation, nor about his or her needs, to bring real issues to the table. Both mentor and mentee rapidly become bored, and the developmental opportunity is lost.

Some schemes now deliberately defer the appointment of a mentor for the first few months, preferring to give the graduate a 'buddy' from a previous intake, who can answer most of the questions about where to find things and how to behave. Mentoring relationships established after this tend to have an immediately higher sense of purpose and quality of dialogue.

3 Linking to competencies

Early thinking on graduate mentoring was that the mentor should avoid discussion on specific competencies because it might undermine the authority of the graduate's line manager. There is, of course, still some truth in that, but the recognition is increasingly that clarity of role between line manager (as coach), mentor and human resources in developing the graduate is essential. The mentor can help the graduate examine specific competency needs beyond the confines of current tasks and in the perspective of his or her career as a whole.

4 Who gets trained?

Early mentoring schemes focused training on the mentors. Most new schemes emphasise the need for the mentee to play a much greater role in managing the relationship. The evidence suggests that the benefits flowing from mentoring increase significantly when both parties fully understand what is expected of them and how they can get the best out of it. Mentee training can be shorter than mentor training, but there are practical skills – such as how to structure requests for help – that can be of particular value to the mentee.

One of the particular benefits reported by mentors from mentee training is that the graduates start the relationship with clearer, more realistic expectations about what the mentor can or should do for them, and about their own responsibilities in maintaining the relationship.

Some companies, such as BAT, also train line manager coaches in the basics of mentoring so that they will be supportive of the role and will be less likely to feel threatened by it.

5 Focus on the practical

A lot of graduate mentoring schemes have floundered because people did not know what to do. Even where they had had some form of training, they lacked the confidence to make the relationship work. Typically, either the mentor or the mentee talked for an hour or so, and both wondered why they were there. Some companies involve the line manager in the first meeting, helping to create some sense of purpose and direction. Others simply provide an opportunity to practise how to conduct the initial and subsequent meetings. Such practice sessions instil confidence and identify concerns that may hinder the successful relationship.

6 Focus on opportunities, not problems

Some mentoring schemes in which I have participated have struggled because the mentor has been presented as 'someone who can help you with your problems'. If the environment is such that it discourages people from discussing their problems with someone more senior (or even admitting they have problems), the pair soon run out of things to talk about. Part of the problem is that mentors often lack the career counselling skills to be of much use in helping the graduate define and seize opportunities. This argues for continued training of mentors as more all-round 'developers of people', and for the involvement of the mentor group as a whole in succession planning and development planning.

7 Review relationships at least twice in the first year

Early schemes simply put people together and hoped for the best. There is now much greater use of matching processes, some utilising software to provide a measure towards an assessment of compatibility. Good practice schemes also allow either mentor or graduate to withdraw if the relationship does not work out, under a 'no fault divorce clause'. Where this is done with a planned, constructive discussion between mentor and graduate, it typically results in a more appropriate second match.

It is also useful to gather feedback from both mentors and graduates at six months and 12 months on the performance of their relationships and the scheme as a whole. This allows the scheme co-ordinator to intervene as necessary, perhaps with specific further training.

8 Gain the commitment of top management

Mentoring has flourished in organisations with a generally poor development climate when it has received public and enthusiastic support from top management. In particular, if top management is prepared to both be mentors to middle managers and to talk about their own experiences as mentees, it provides an impetus to the whole programme.

9 Recognising and supporting the mentors

One of the most common concerns expressed by graduate mentors is that even having been trained, they are largely left to it. Sir John Harvey-Jones says that one of the few things he wished he had done differently at ICI was to make a bigger deal of the efforts of senior people as mentors. Some companies now reward mentors by making them members of 'development clubs' which have greater than normal access to directors and their thinking – knowledge that is, of course, very useful in discussions with graduates about career direction.

10 The two-year cliff edge

Within the typical two-year duration of the graduate mentoring scheme, the relationship generally winds down. The graduate is settled into the organisation, has become part of a normal work team, and has a reasonable idea of where he or she is headed. He or she does not really need a mentor any more, and in that mentors are a scarce resource, the relationship is usually expected to come to an end.

What frequently happens after the two years, however, is that the graduate begins to acquire greater responsibilities which provide a whole new set of challenges, or gets bored because the challenges do not come fast enough. In either situation there is high potential for this valuable resource to be lured away.

Enter the secondary mentor, someone usually more senior than the first, whose role is to help the graduate – now an employee without a special label on his or her collar – to continue to develop a career within the organisation. This mentor is likely to be more challenging, better networked and sometimes more demanding than the first. This 'layering' of levels of mentor is becoming an increasingly common characteristic of organisations which wish to maximise their use of a scarce developmental resource.

GRADUATE MENTORING IN THE NEXT DECADE

The rapid improvements in effectiveness of graduate mentoring schemes is set to continue. Among innovations already here or on the way are upward mentoring (GE's Jack Welch and his top team were all mentored by young computer whizzes, to keep them up to date); mentoring training delivered online; e-mentoring; improved processes to link career/ succession planning with mentoring; and better systems to measure the outputs of mentoring relationships. There are, however, still a fair number of schemes that operate on the principles of the late 1980s – these will come under increasing pressure to change, not least because graduates themselves compare notes across employers.

Just having a graduate mentoring scheme will no longer be enough to attract and keep talent. Graduates are increasingly demanding proof that the process works, that it delivers real benefits, and that it will genuinely facilitate the achievement of their career goals.

SUMMARY

From being the most common form of mentoring in organisations, graduate mentoring has become one of many applications. However, pressure form graduate recruits is making employers conscious that their graduate mentoring programmes have to be much more effective than has normally been the case.

CASE STUDY

UBS Graduate Mentoring Programme

The Graduate and High-Potentials Mentoring Programme at UBS Warburg in the UK started in 1999. The aim of the programme is for mentees to develop self-reliance and self-awareness. The mentors are used as role models and offer advice, allowing the mentees to have a series of options around their development. The programme also aids recruitment and retention within the organisation.

Details of the scheme

- There is initial research into the marketplace.
- A search is undertaken for a provider that enables independence between the mentee and the business unit he or she is operating in.
- All mentors and mentees must attend a workshop where ground rules and confidentiality are clarified.
- The mentor must be one corporate title above the mentee.
- The mentor must be in a different business unit.
- The matching process is carried out by independent line development officers.

Measurement

- Measurement of workshop effectiveness is carried out via 'happy sheets'.
- Satisfaction surveys have shown that 85 per cent of delegates are very satisfied with the programme.
- The programme has proved most effective around personal development issues and career planning.

Key things to do in setting up a programme, as learned from the UBS case

- Get senior management commitment.
- Clarify ground rules and expectations up front.
- Clarify the matching process.

Mentees are encouraged to become mentors and are also expected to become buddies to new entrants.

CASE STUDY

The National Graduate Development Programme for local government

The NGDP was launched in September 2002 as part of the local government sector's drive to recruit and retain high-calibre young people. One of the four key elements of the programme – along with placements within a local authority, National Training events and a Warwick Business School Diploma – is an External Mentoring Programme.

The National Management Trainees (NMTs) are matched up with senior managers from within the sector but outside of their host authority. 'This is a unique opportunity,' said Jill Martin, the co-ordinator of the programme, 'because it means we can provide the NMTs with a valuable source of support and insight external to their own organisation – something that most other sectors would find it difficult to provide.'

The purpose of external mentoring, which focuses on the second year of the two-year programme, was to encourage the trainees to view their roles from a wider perspective and to formulate post-programme career plans.

Identifying this purpose and the criteria by which its achievement would be measured was the vital first step in setting up the mentoring programme. The next step was to determine ideal mentor criteria. 'Although seniority and experience is important, self-awareness and commitment to their personal learning and development were most critical,' said Jill. 'Potential mentors were asked to provide evidence via a questionnaire against the selection criteria.'

Suitable mentors were then invited to attend regional 'information days', which combined training, clarification of expectations and discussions about how to maximise the success of the programme. The trainees participated in similar sessions at their National Training events, which also stressed their own responsibilities as mentees.

Relating to a national programme, the key matching criterion was geographical location. However, meeting all the mentors and mentees has also played an important part in the matching process. 'It might seem subjective but we are confident that this approach will be a success.'

Although the mentoring programme is still in its infancy, a great deal has already been learned. For example, it was decided to delay the initial launch of the programme by six months to ensure that the best possible mentors could participate, all of whom had attended an information day before meeting their mentee. This may have caused some concerns for the trainees in the short term, but in the long term quality was more important than hitting a deadline.

It has also been interesting to note that people have put themselves forward as mentors for many different reasons. 'The ones we have most confidence in are those with the desire to learn from their mentee and who see the programme as a development opportunity for both parties rather than purely to put something back into local government.'

14

Diversity mentoring

When I first wrote *Everyone Needs a Mentor*, the concept of using mentoring as a vehicle for promoting equal opportunity was still fairly new. The handful of programmes there were tended to focus on high-potential women. Since then, several evolutions have occurred. One is that mentoring for equal opportunity at work now addresses a wide range of target groups, from women at all levels and career stages, through ethnic minorities, to the mentally and physically disabled. The other is that the concept of equal opportunity has to a significant extent been overtaken by diversity management. Where equal opportunity attempts to redress the power-balance in the workplace in favour of previously disadvantaged groups, diversity management takes the more positivist view that organisations should be making the maximum use of the diversity of cultures, skills, genders and personalities within them.

These two views, which are not necessarily incompatible, tend to inform how companies design their mentoring programmes. For many, the most practical approach is a programme aimed specifically at a clearly defined group. Aer Rianta, the Irish Airports Authority, achieved significant results over a number of years with a programme to link women in junior and middle management with male executives (there were no female executives at the time). An Post, the Irish Post Office, recently embarked on a similar scheme, but using mentors drawn from key customers and suppliers. The problems with such an approach, however, include:

- There is the possibility that many potential participants do not want to be labelled in this way, as BP Engineering found when it consulted a cross-section of its female employees. Rather, they wanted to be encouraged to join a wider scheme, open to all, which would not carry the stigma of disadvantage.

- There is the difficulty of defining just who is disadvantaged (is a black female with an Oxbridge education more disadvantaged than a white male with a poor education and from a lower-class background?) and who belongs to a group. One North American company was embarrassed when homosexual employees complained that the women's leadership programme disadvantaged them, so the company formed another scheme, only to find that other groups, such as the physically disabled, also wanted the same privileges. Confused by a plethora of schemes, potential mentors backed away in droves. The company attempted to place all the disadvantaged groups into one scheme, but some groups did not want to be categorised alongside others they considered different. The process collapsed under the weight of bureaucracy and now anyone, from any group, including the most positively advantaged, can apply for a mentor.

- How valid are the assumptions about behavioural change? For example, a gender-based glass ceiling programme defined its mentoring element in terms of helping women understand how to think and behave at a more senior level. Some of the women challenged this definition and asked for an analysis of what behaviours they needed to acquire. It soon became clear that cloning male executives might not meet the programme goal because a high proportion of the male executives did not exemplify these behaviours either. Indeed, in many cases the female mentees were better exemplars of those behaviours than their intended mentors. Redefining the programme to legitimise building on the strengths the women had, rather than to change them into something else, gave a stronger sense of commitment and purpose.

Mentoring aimed to support diversity management overcomes most of these problems, but it makes it much more difficult to target mentoring on people who will particularly benefit from it. Companies taking this approach tend to develop practical methods to encourage people to come forward – for example, by making mentoring an option to be considered at each performance appraisal.

SAME GROUP, DIFFERENT GROUP?

One of the most controversial issues in diversity mentoring is whether the mentor should be from the same group or a different group.

A strong practical reason against same-group mentoring in many organisations is that there are not enough people from the minority or disadvantaged group to meet the demand. Because two or at most three mentees per mentor is the maximum recommended, there will frequently be a supply-and-demand problem. One of the major mistakes organisations make is to press into service the handful of senior managers who are black or female (or both), regardless of whether they have the aptitude and interest to be an active and effective mentor.

There seem to be five key aspects to the arguments around this issue.

The first is *perspective* – whether and how the mentor can help the mentee view his or her issues in a manner useful to learning. The mentor from a different group – especially if he or she is also at a higher level in the organisation – can provide a very different set of viewpoints. If the mentor comes from the powerful majority, he or she may be better at explaining how the system functions and how to work with it rather than against it. The mentor is able to help the mentee see barriers and opportunities in ways that make them easier to tackle.

For example, a young Muslim mentee was having great difficulty adapting to working in a multinational organisation. He expected to be given frequent, clear instructions and to report back to his supervisor constantly. Instead, he found that the supervisor responded with:

'Look, you know what to do. Why don't you just get on with it?' As a result, relationships between them were very strained, especially when the mentee was passed over for a promotion. Working with the mentor, this young man gradually came to understand what the supervisor's expectations were and the value the organisation placed upon self-reliance and demonstrating initiative. He also worked out how to fit in with the organisation's behavioural expectations, while not sacrificing any of the values important to him from his own culture. He rehearsed with the mentor how he would discuss these issues with his supervisor to build a better understanding between them.

Whereas a difference of perspective was important here, in other cases the dominant need may be for greater empathy. The white mentor above could not easily put himself in the mentee's shoes – he had never been in such a situation. Same-group mentors can extend greater understanding. One of the classic examples is the experiment by part of the Prudential in the UK to assist returning mothers with a mentor. The mentor – a mum who had made the same transition within recent years – contacted the employee some months ahead of the return date and worked with her for several months until she had settled back in again. The mentor in this case was able to share the feelings of guilt, inadequacy and being pulled in too many directions, which so many returning mothers feel. 'Being able to talk with someone who had been there and come through it made all the difference,' said one mentee.

The second key aspect is *networking*. The mentor from the dominant group is likely to be much better connected, and even a mentor who is not in the power structure will be able to introduce the mentee to very different people. The same-group mentor is likely to have networks that largely overlap with those of the mentee.

Power is the third aspect. Minority-group mentors are less likely to be in senior positions, so they cannot provide either the depth of understanding of the organisation (another result of perspective) or – in sponsorship mentoring – the potential to exert influence on the mentee's behalf. If the mentee is ambitious, there is much to be learned from someone who has developed the skills of acquiring and using power wisely.

Being a role model is also an important consideration. Same-group mentors may be more likely to reinforce attitudes and behaviours that are not valued by the organisation. Different-group mentors can provide role models for behaviours that are valued. (However, it may not always be possible for the mentee to distinguish between appropriate and inappropriate role models – having a mentor from both groups may provide greater insight.)

In deciding whether the relationship should be constructed within the same group or across different groups, then, a variety of issues has to be taken into account. The most fundamental, however, is *what is the mentee's need?* If support is the most critical need, then a same-group mentor may be most appropriate. If being stretched is the goal, then a mentor from a different group is likely to be most effective. In addition, it should be remembered that the mentor is not the only potential source of learning for the mentee – the wider the learning net the mentee can create, the more he or she can receive of both nurture and challenge.

POSITIONING DIVERSITY

The increasing numbers of women and minorities now entering careers in management suffer from a major disadvantage – by and large they are not exposed to the same range of experiences and career opportunities as men. Although formal barriers have been reduced through legislation, women and minority groups continue to be hindered in their careers by invisible obstacles such as prejudice and distrust. As the demand for high-quality white-collar management increases, the need for organisations to question why there are so few women and minorities in management will become acute.

When these managers *are* accepted in the formal structure of the organisation, in the informal social structure they can *still* be looked on with suspicion. For example, the masculine culture of a company may mean that women are not fully integrated; in a sense they are still regarded as outsiders or interlopers.

Low expectations or stereotyped images can often mean that women and minority managers are delegated undemanding jobs, making them less visible than white male managers. Women may be expected to perform tasks that are seen as suitably 'feminine' in nature, such as personnel, rather than the more 'masculine' managerial jobs, such as financial analysis. As a result, women managers frequently lack opportunities to develop a wide range of managerial skills.

In the UK some years ago I carried out a survey of businesswomen, using questionnaires sent to 100 who had reached executive level inside a company and to 100 women entrepreneurs. The response rate was a remarkable 49 per cent. Among the key conclusions were:

- Successful women managers are more likely than women entrepreneurs to have had a mentor (56 per cent compared with 43 per cent). One reason – possibly the most important – is that the entrepreneuses quit to set up on their own precisely because their progress was blunted in large corporations, through lack of a champion at higher levels.

- Forty-nine per cent of the women had had a single mentor; 22 per cent had had two; 21 per cent had had three; and 8 per cent had had four or five – or more – at different periods in their careers.

- Ninety-four per cent of the women who had mentors said their relationships were beneficial to their career.

- More than half of the entrepreneuses' mentors had encouraged them to start their own businesses; 5 per cent even helped them financially.

- The vast majority of mentoring relationships (63 per cent) started accidentally; only 8 per cent of the women had actually approached their mentor.

- The main benefits reported by the women were:
  - improved self-confidence and self-image
  - increased visibility to senior management (especially important to women managers)
  - focusing career aspirations
  - acting as a role model
  - help with work problems
  - improved communications and skills.
- Most mentors (79 per cent) were male.
- More than two-fifths experienced no problems with the relationship; 37 per cent had experienced problems of resentment from peers; 5 per cent said their careers had been damaged when their mentor lost credibility in the company.
- Two-thirds had experienced some form of sexual innuendo or gossip; 19 per cent reported that their mentor's wife felt threatened by the relationship; 11 per cent said their own husbands resented it; 4 per cent said their mentor became too emotionally involved with them.
- Sixty per cent of the women were acting as mentors themselves.

Dr Judi Marshall of Bath University found that mentoring improved the promotion prospects of women managers. Interviewing 30 women managers from middle management to director level, Marshall found that 70 per cent either were currently or had been in a mentoring relationship. All of these women placed great value on the relationship and said it had been a very important factor in their career development. The majority of the women saw visibility as a crucial factor for success. The mentors sponsored the women and often nominated them for promotion committees when they would not have normally been considered for posts. If a mentor vouches for a woman manager, companies are more willing to promote her because they view the mentor as a 'safety net', Marshall concludes.

Jenny Blake, an independent consultant, comments:

I think the mentoring relationship is very beneficial to both the mentee and the mentor. In my capacity as a consultant I now try to fill the mentor role. I mentor personnel trainers and help them with their own development. At the moment I am mentoring a senior manager in the probationary service. I feel an older woman can play a very positive role as a mentor. I do not appear threatening to men, so I receive open feedback. I have found that an increasing number of women in their late thirties and forties are now willing to be mentors. They want to act as a role model to younger women to demonstrate that women can succeed in business. It seems clear to me that mentoring can and will play a very positive role in the future.

Potential problems with male/female mentoring

Between the mentee and the mentor

A female mentee often experiences disappointment with the relationship because her male mentor is unable to meet all her developmental needs. She cannot emulate him fully, and in certain areas may need to find her own methods of achieving goals and resolving problems. Women put more emphasis than men on delegating or on group discussion. If the male mentor does not understand this, he may interpret it as lack of assertiveness and push the female mentee into signing up for an assertiveness course.

Sexual tensions between the two can inhibit the relationship and make it less rewarding than mentoring between two of the same sex.

Pressure to adopt established sexual roles sometimes causes tension and conflict in the relationship. A male mentor may feel overly protective towards a female mentor and encourage her to be dependent. She may find it particularly difficult to terminate the relationship at the end of the mentoring programme. The same may also be true in the case of a female mentor and male mentee, especially where the age differences are similar to those in a mother/son relationship.

Says Dr Marilyn Puder-York, a clinical psychologist in New York:

> There are many very productive male-female mentoring relationships, but there must be a high sense of shared values and ethical behaviour on both sides. And you often have to counter society's perception of the relationship by having lunch instead of dinner and by including spouses in socialising. Otherwise both can pay a heavy price. In general, if a woman has a male mentor, she should seek out a woman mentor as well. Beyond the social considerations, there are politics for women that a man may not be aware of.

Between the spouses and the mentoring pair

A mentoring relationship can seem threatening to the mentor's and mentee's partners, especially if business trips together are involved. The spouse often feels excluded by the closeness of the relationship.

Mentees have found various solutions, mostly based on total openness. Social gatherings to which spouses are invited make a useful opportunity to demonstrate the businesslike nature of the relationship.

Between the company and the mentoring pair

Sexual gossip and innuendo can kill a mentoring relationship before it gets going. Many potential male/female mentoring relationships never happen because of the fear of office gossip. In a mentoring programme it is often necessary for the two to work beyond work hours or even travel together. The two must act 'professionally', which can simply mean that behaviour has to be much more circumscribed than in a mentor relationship between two of the same sex. One mentor solved the problem of gossip:

If you mentor one woman you are branded as a womaniser. If you mentor several, you are praised for your commitment to seeing more women in management.

The extra visibility of the relationship in the company may discourage even the highest risk-taker from being a mentor: 'A young man can have the luxury of failing quietly, but a woman's mistakes are often broadcast,' explains one mentor.

MENTORING ACROSS RACIAL/CULTURAL DIVIDES

Mentoring between races requires equally sensitive handling. The potential for stereotyping to reduce the effectiveness of the relationship is high – as too is the potential to identify and overcome stereotypes. In experiments across cultures I have found it is important to begin the relationship with an extra dose of clarity about expectations. On one occasion, in Brunei, managers being trained as mentors were asked to plot the shape of the relationship in terms of where the emphasis of behaviours should rest. Figure 15 shows what the expatriate (English and Dutch) mentors concluded.

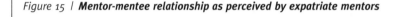

Figure 15 | *Mentor-mentee relationship as perceived by expatriate mentors*

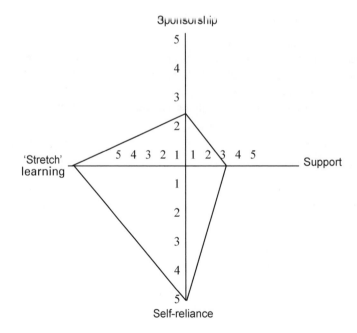

Figure 16 shows what the mentees, who were mostly local people in their mid-twenties, were expecting.

*Figure 16 | **Mentor-mentee relationship as perceived by mentees abroad***

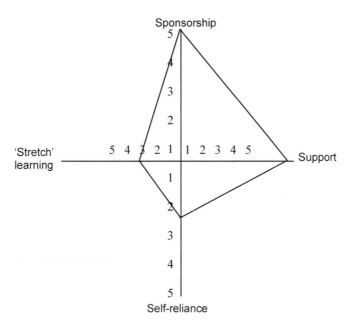

On seeing these diagrams and after nearly two minutes of silence, one manager exclaimed, 'Now I see why I have such difficulty getting through to my direct reports!' Mentors and mentees used this information to discuss what behaviours and expectations on both sides would be appropriate, and to build a compromise acceptable to both parties.

Like mentoring across genders, mentoring across cultures is an excellent developmental experience for the mentor. Some companies now encourage such relationships as an integral part of globalising their cultures.

CASE STUDY

London Borough of Brent – Mentoring for a diverse workforce

Sue Gover and Marianne Ecker

During 2001, the London Borough of Brent launched a series of initiatives under the banner of an 'Improving Brent' programme. This focused on both personal and service improvement while at the same time converging with the requirements of the Campaign for Racial Equality's Action Plan.

One initiative introduced under the 'Improving Brent' umbrella was a 12-month mentoring scheme aimed initially at black and Asian staff. The stated aims of the scheme were:

- to encourage a more proactive approach to learning and move further towards becoming a learning organisation
- to enable individuals to be more self-reliant through improved career and personal/professional development that would encourage them actively to take responsibility for their actions
- to provide a development opportunity for individuals who had not been able to take part in other development initiatives
- to enable individuals to have a greater understanding of the work pressures and priorities outside their own area, providing them with a Council-wide view
- to support the new Council-wide appraisal process, where there was now an opportunity to discuss training and learning in general
- to ensure that the management structure reflected the makeup of the whole population at the Council.

The scheme began with a manageable 25 pairs, all of whom attended a one-day formal training programme. During training, personal portfolios were filled out and then used, in conjunction with the initial application forms, to do the matching.

Uniquely, the scheme was actively supported by a steering group of four people, based in different locations around the Borough and thus well-placed to help participants. Besides providing support to individuals, the role of the group was to oversee implementation of the scheme, and particularly the matching and evaluation processes.

Feedback was obtained twice during the course of the year and also at the conclusion of the formal relationships. A creditable 79 per cent of participants felt that their expectations had been met. This and other feedback was shared at an open day run by the steering group and supported by the Borough directorate. Comments made by mentees included: 'My mentor makes me think and see things through', 'Beliefs and differences were accepted, and I was able to speak openly', 'It made me feel special and that someone was listening', 'It removed preconceived barriers', 'You get what you put in', and 'My mentor's insights helped me acquire the knowledge I wanted about the unit I wanted to work in.'

For each of the three different stakeholder groups, the perceived benefits of mentoring were that:

mentors

- gained insights into the work of parts of the organisation with which they did not come into direct contact – assisting in organisational integration and communication

- experienced more closely the challenges facing employees and the impact of senior management decisions on the organisation

- were able to change their own mindsets and share learning with others

- gained an opportunity to examine their own style and improve management of their own employees

mentees

- gained an opportunity to discuss career and development aspirations with a more senior member of staff from another service area

- had a confidant(e) with whom to explore current work problems and resolutions

- were able to see a range of management styles and techniques

Brent, the organisation

- improved the development and progression of black and Asian staff

- assisted in identifying potential, particularly for management roles

- increased the identification and development of key competencies

- promoted the transfer of skills, leading to motivation and productivity

- became a source of feedback on how key organisational processes were working, such as recruitment and selection.

The steering group's purpose in holding an open day was twofold: firstly, to share with participants and others the outcomes from the first year of mentoring, and secondly, to provide a forum for prospective new participants to hear at first hand what mentoring was about and how it worked in Brent.

The success of the first year's scheme was such that a second phase was launched towards the end of 2002. This was open to all staff, a percentage of places being held for positive-action candidates. Built into this next phase were the key learning points drawn out by the steering group from Phase 1:

Initial application phase:

- Improve communication about the programme by using the intranet and attending team meetings; launch the next programme with an open seminar, celebrating success of this programme.

- Involve the line managers – ask them to sign mentees' application forms and arrange a briefing session specifically for them.

- Extend the opportunity to all staff, while retaining a number of positive-action places.

Training:

- Spend more time on clarifying roles, expectations and the level of commitment required; explain the evaluation process; emphasise that building rapport is key and can take time; focus on building/achieving medium-term objectives (*v* short-term).

Matching:

- It takes a lot of time; the more information you can get from participants, the better; limit the number of hierarchical levels between mentor and mentee.

Implementation:

- Some people need help and support in getting started.
- Give good practice guidelines – eg on how often and how long to meet for.
- Offer occasional workshops to support mentees, such as on interview skills.
- Now give more emphasis to mentor development during the year, to help them move mentees to consider medium-term objectives.

Organisational learning:

- To illustrate the relationship between mentoring and improved performance, change over time must be tracked.
- There are strong links between mentor skills and general management skills.
- There is a need to build on the gains for individuals.
- We must offer more than just access to mentoring to help BME staff progress – they need practical management experience to make them credible candidates for their first management posts – we should be looking now to provide shadowing and other tools to facilitate this.

Mentoring is now perceived as an important building-block in the 'Improving Brent' programme, and it continues to thrive and be supported by the steering group.

SUMMARY

Mentoring for diversity is one of the most positive developments in organisational learning in recent years. It benefits the disadvantaged employee, for whom doors begin to open up; it benefits the mentor, who learns how to interact with and get the most from employees of widely differing backgrounds; and it benefits the company by making much more effective use of the talent available.

15

Executive mentoring

One area in which mentoring has grown very rapidly has been at the very top of organisations. Although a few companies, such as engineers T&N, have experimented with peer mentoring between directors, and others, such as Diageo, have developed a cadre of HR professionals whose main role is to coach and/or mentor the top hundred or so people, most mentoring of executives and directors is carried out by external mentors, who are often professionals in the role.

THE GROWING POPULARITY OF EXECUTIVE MENTORING

So why has executive mentoring suddenly become so popular? Among the stimuli for the executive mentoring movement are (Clutterbuck and Schneider, 1998):

- There has been *a gradual repositioning of the nature and role of mentoring* at this level. The UK, along with most other Western nations, has a tradition of high-level mentoring with strong sponsorship overtones. As you set your sights on the executive suite, you seek an elder statesperson who can actively steer your progress, find opportunities that will increase your visibility, make introductions and generally be influential on your behalf. Because most people prefer to be seen as having succeeded by their own efforts, it is hardly surprising that they were sometimes reluctant to acknowledge the mentor's role and contribution.

- *The rapid spread of developmental mentoring* in the past ten years, especially among graduates and minorities, has gradually changed the perception of mentoring in general – at least in the UK and Europe. This is much more in keeping with the image executives are comfortable to project, especially when they are expected to be a role model to others.

- At the same time, there is *an increasing acceptance that development is a continuous, career-long activity*, even (perhaps especially) at the top. Time pressures make it very difficult for executives to attend business school seminars frequently, and much of the training provided both in such courses and within their organisations is at too low a level to be immediately relevant to their needs. Executives learn most intensively from working on real issues, business or personal, in small groups or one-to-one.

- *The nature of executive roles has changed.* Senior managers and directors operate in an increasingly complex and stressful environment. Constant organisational change demands constant personal change at the top. For the executive to maintain his or her pace of personal change alongside that of the organisation, he or she needs someone else who can goad, support, ask penetrating questions and be a kind of 'development conscience'. This is particularly true in smaller businesses, where a major cause of failure is that the business grows faster than the capabilities of the owner-entrepreneur to manage it.

- *Organisation structures have also been changing.* With flatter hierarchies, the transition from middle to senior manager, or senior manager to director, has become much more of a shock to the system. The learning curve is very steep and anecdotal evidence suggests that, for example, fewer than one in three people who take on the title of director fully absorb the difference in role. Having someone help you through these major transitions is becoming almost a necessity.

Professional mentors help executives get at their own issues, build their own insights and self-awareness, and develop their own, unique ways of handling how they interact with key colleagues and with the business. The professional mentor uses current issues to explore patterns of thinking and behaviour, often starting with the executive's values. He or she asks penetrating questions that stimulate thinking, challenges the executive to take control of issues avoided, helps the executive put his or her own learning in context and raise his or her ability to cope with new issues through greater self-understanding and confidence.

To be effective, professional mentors have to have a broad knowledge and exposure to business direction, to the patterns of senior management thinking and behaviour. They must have a store of relevant business, strategic and behavioural models – and the capacity to generate bespoke models on the spot – which can help executives explore the context of issues under discussion. They need exceptional interpersonal skills of their own, together with a more than passing competence in what can broadly be called counselling skills. Not surprisingly, these are relatively rare creatures.

One reason professional mentoring is so much more demanding – on the executive as well as the mentor – is that it is so holistic. It seeks and deals with issues wherever they are. It requires the mentor to recognise and adapt roles according to the executive's needs at the time. So the mentor may need to be coach, counsellor, sounding-board, critical friend, networker, or any of a number of roles, sometimes within the same two-hour session. This constant reassessing and refocusing is helped by addressing the executive's issues from at least three viewpoints – the values and emotions that drive their behaviour and decision-making, the leader-manager style they adopt, and the needs of the business. Among key questions that emerge frequently are (Clutterbuck and Schneider, 1998):

- How do you think about this issue? (Is your thinking rigorous enough? Adventurous enough?)

- What do you feel about the issue?

- How does this make you behave? (And how consistent is your behaviour?)

- How do you make things happen? (And what do you do when they do not happen?)

- How well do you understand what is really going on in your team? Your business?

- How well do you understand what happens within you? (Do you need to develop greater self-awareness? Can you increase your 'emotional intelligence'?)

- How could you contribute more (not just in the business, but to your own well-being and that of other people)?

IN-HOUSE OR EXTERNAL MENTOR?

The cost of professional external mentors is enough to make most companies think twice about large-scale provision. In general, an external mentor is most appropriate when:

- the executive would find it difficult to be sufficiently open to an insider

- he or she is looking to tap into specific expertise or experience not available within the company.

Internal mentors are most appropriate when:

- there is a strong culture of peer dialogue and open learning

- the top team contains good role models for mentoring behaviours

- a knowledge of the internal politics and the organisation is important to the relationship.

In general, it pays to take the view that a good case needs to be made for external provision, and to make it clear that having an external mentor is not a status symbol, or a reward for good service, but a response to a specifically defined need. It is also important to be sure that a mentor is what is needed, rather than an executive coach or specialist counselling.

An external coach is most appropriate if:

- the need is remedial or to do with a specific skill set (eg delegation rather than leadership in general)

- the relationship is intended to be a short-term intervention (ie six months or less)

- achieving the developmental objective is likely to require direct observation and feedback by the external resource.

(There is considerable debate at the moment about how different the roles of coach and mentor are in the context of professional external provision. Although it is true that many of the same skill sets are required and there are well-trained practitioners who can bridge the two roles, the mentee or coachee must be quite clear as to the nature and scope of the relationship.)

Counselling is normally an option when the executive's performance issues are related to deeper psychological issues, rather than to technique. Again, there is considerable debate about the need for competence in behavioural psychology on the part of the coach or mentor. Stephen Berglas, in a controversial article in *Harvard Business Review* (June 2002), maintains that all coaches (he does not refer to mentors) should be psychologists, on the grounds that failure to spot psychoses leads to inappropriate guidance and sometimes to harm for the client. Other sources counter with the argument that few psychologists have the business or commercial understanding to be able to empathise with and contextualise the majority of problems that executives face. The answer seems to lie somewhere in between – to be effective in the role, professional executive coaches and mentors need a grounding in both psychology and management at a senior level.

Selecting the external mentor

Companies we are working with are increasingly setting up panels of approved coaches and mentors with sufficient breadth in composition to meet a variety of needs by their executives. This allows them, for example, to link an executive who is leading his first merger with an 'elder statesman' who has been through the same mill numerous times, and to provide the potential director who needs to acquire learning on a number of fronts with a much more broadly skilled mentor who has a stronger background in behavioural psychology.

Each of these companies has established an interview template, which it uses to assess potential external mentors and coaches. It also makes sense to bring together the active mentors/coaches at least twice a year to discuss, within the bounds of client confidentiality, their observations about the organisation. Their perceptions can be invaluable in identifying cultural and broad developmental issues that the organisation needs to address. The panel members also gain peer learning, an important part of their continuous professional development (CPD). Some companies have decided that mentors and coaches who do not participate in these sessions should be dropped from the panel – not least because involvement in CPD is a key competence for the role.

CASE STUDY

Discovery – an executive mentoring programme in Norway

Jennybeth Ekeland

A society which does not educate and train its women is like a person who just trains the right arm.

(Plato, BC 427–347)

Discovery is a mentoring programme aimed at increasing the number of women in high-level executive positions in Norway. The NHO (Norwegian Federation for Business and Industry) started the programme in 1996; in 1999 AFF (the Norwegian School of Economics and Business Administration) took over the programme. Since then 760 people – 380 mentees and the same number of mentors – have participated in the programme.

The mentees come from large Norwegian organisations, mostly from finance, media, IT and manufacturing. The age of the mentees ranges from 28 to 57. They all have experience as managers, some at a very high executive level. In recent years, the programme has been open to men as well, but few have taken the opportunity.

The mentors are top-level senior executives. Most of them are men, but the proportion of women is increasing. At first each company selected both mentors and mentees for the programme. Because the quality of the mentoring relationship greatly depends on the capability of the mentor, AFF changed this procedure. Today all the mentors are hand-picked to meet the developing needs of the mentees.

AFF finds the mentors from its network of senior executives who have attended leadership programmes over the years since 1952. These people see the role as continuing their own leadership development as mentors. The mentors are not paid for the work – this is a Norwegian mentoring tradition!

About the programme

When the companies have selected mentees, the project co-ordinators conduct comprehensive interviews in order to match mentor and mentees.

Discovery is a one-year programme. During this year there are four kinds of formal meeting or seminar:

- One half-day seminar to begin with, at which all the mentors and mentees meet together. The purpose is to establish a good working environment for the mentoring process. We focus on what mentoring is and the role of the mentor and mentee. There is also some training in mentoring skills.

- Meetings for the mentees. One month after the start, the mentees meet for networking and to clarify their roles.

- At four months and eight months there is a one-day meeting of both mentors and mentees for networking and sharing experience. Some additional training in mentoring skills is also included.

- At the end of the year everybody meets for a half-day seminar that includes dinner, to summarise the learning and to celebrate what they have received!

During the year every mentor and mentee has a minimum of ten to twelve meetings, each of 1½ to 2 hours. Both mentee and mentor must be committed to the programme and its goals, and make active participation a priority.

The mentors and mentees are also included in AFF's networking arrangements. They are invited to five half-day management seminars within the year, and receive AFF's newsletter which contains updated articles about leadership and organisational development.

In recent years the programme co-ordinator has co-operated with Clutterbuck Associates in developing the programme and in using the the Mentoring Dynamics Survey (an instrument diagnostic of relationship quality, which also acts as a stimulus for reflection on the progress of the relationship).

Evaluation

Each segment of the programme is evaluated to assess both processes and outcomes. During the evaluation, assessment data is monitored to check:

- that both mentors and mentees are learning(!)
- that both report
- increased self-insight
- increased self-confidence
- better understanding and consciousness of the leadership role
- greater awareness of values and attitudes
- increased work satisfaction.

One of the aims of the programme is to help develop stronger networks – and this is the one disappointing area in our evaluations, for relatively few participants make significant use of this opportunity. Participants seem to put all their efforts into the mentor-mentee relationship itself. We suspect this is in part an issue of the Norwegian culture – other research undertaken by AFF shows that Norwegians often underestimate the importance of networking.

A Discovery programme for the regional districts of Norway

Inspired by Discovery, SND (the Norwegian Industrial and Regional Development Foundation) initiated a mentoring programme in 2000 for the regional districts of Norway. It was given the name LeaderMentor because the programme contains more leadership development elements than Discovery does. The participants hail from anywhere between the furthest south and the furthest north of Norway. A majority of the mentees come from very small enterprises, and the SND lends some economic support to their participation. It is an extra-difficult challenge for the AFF then to try to match mentors with mentees who enjoy some degree of geographical proximity.

The steering committee

AFF, NHO and SND have together set up a steering committee to look after the development of these two programmes. The committee has six members who not only are very experienced and prominent in the mentoring field but are also top-level senior executives – and all have been mentors or mentees. The steering committee plays an important and powerful role in the development of the mentoring programmes of the AFF.

SUMMARY

Executive mentoring is a rapidly expanding area of practice. Most activity occurs through external provision, not least because senior managers find it hard to open themselves to peers who may also be rivals for the top jobs. It is quite difficult for many executives to admit their fears and weaknesses to colleagues. A few companies, such as Diageo, have experimented with internal specialists – usually people with a strong behavioural psychology background who operate with a high degree of independence. However, it is hard to develop the depth of friendship that typifies the really effective mentoring relationship. For those who venture outside the organisation, there is no shortage of willing providers. But there is often confusion between executive coaching (building a particular skill set) and executive mentoring (thinking through issues more deeply). Moreover, there are no barriers to entry and no widely subscribed set of professional standards. *Caveat emptor*!

16

E-mentoring

e-mentoring: mentoring relationships conducted primarily or entirely via e-mail

I am, I have to admit, a converted sceptic about mentoring at a distance. Having invested so much time and research into the virtues of face-to-face developmental dialogue, I could not see how the mentoring relationship could possibly be as meaningful when the primary form of communication was e-mail. Experience as an e-mentor and interviews with participants in successful e-mentoring relationships have convinced me that e-mentoring is not an inferior substitute for 'real' mentoring. Rather, it is simply a different approach to mentoring and can be as effective – and in some cases, potentially more effective – than traditional approaches.

The arguments against e-mentoring can be summarised as follows:

- Even with teleconferencing, it is much more difficult to recognise the undertones in what someone is saying. With e-mail, you miss hesitations, prevarications and revealing facial expressions.

- Face-to-face dialogue has an immediacy that allows the two people to bounce ideas off each other creatively – it is easier to get into 'flow' when interaction is supported by non-verbal communication.

- Close visual contact allows mentors to use techniques of mirroring to build rapport.

- Words on paper can often be misleading – face-to-face, it is easier to explore what each party understands by a word or phrase.

- Distant communication often leads to a heavy focus on transactional exchanges rather than on relationship-building. This tends to make the relationship shallower. (We have no objective evidence one way or another on this, and not a great deal of anecdotal evidence either, but it is a view strongly held in some quarters.)

- It is more difficult to use techniques such as transactional analysis or NLP, which rely on a range of visual and auditory clues, to help the mentee explore his or her drives, motivations and fears.

However, the contra-arguments are equally convincing:

- Given an issue in writing, mentors are able to spend more time thinking about the advice they give and the questions they will ask. The quality of BDQs ('bloody difficult questions') often improves with e-mentoring. In effect, mentors ask fewer but more succinct and more insight-provoking questions than in the heat of a face-to-face dialogue.

- Equally, mentees have more time to consider their responses. Strong reflectors (in learning styles jargon) particularly appreciate this space. For strong activists it provides a useful discipline to stop and think an issue through.

- Nuances that may be missed in the heat of face-to-face dialogue often become more obvious in text.

- Textual dialogue is easier to review – it is like having a transcript – and mentors report that they often spot patterns or repetitions that they would not otherwise have noticed.

- E-mentoring often allows for much more rapid responses by the mentor to the mentee's urgent enquiries. While it may take several weeks to fix up a suitable time to meet face-to-face, an e-mail exchange can take place the same day or at worst within a few days.

- Whereas a face-to-face mentoring session may take a focused period of a couple of hours, e-mentoring dialogue can be broken down into shorter, progressive exchanges, spread over several days or more.

Like most other approaches within mentoring, e-mentoring clearly has more useful application in some circumstances than in others. Where mentor and mentee are geographically separated, especially if they are in different countries or even different time zones, it provides a practical way of ensuring frequency of interaction between mentor and mentee.

Relatively little e-mentoring is carried out in real time, involving mentor and mentee both seated at the computer at the same time. Most people find that it is more practical, in such circumstances, to use the telephone or video-conferencing.

In practice, most use of e-mentoring is hybrid. Mentoring pairs may meet perhaps once a quarter face-to-face and several times in between by e-mail. Distant pairs may communicate some of the time by e-mail, but at other times by telephone or video-conferencing, to maintain the emotional rapport.

In order to make the best of e-mentoring, it makes sense to consider what the co-ordinator and the participants should do at each stage of the relationship. At the *rapport-building* stage the difficulty is to create a relationship in the first place. Says Kevin Hunt, who organised a large-scale e-mentoring project for small businesses (see case study below):

> *Within the context of mentoring, the relationship is normally one that forms naturally. However, within e-mentoring, creating the relationship early on is absolutely critical. So for large-scale e-mentoring projects the ability to match individuals electronically, when they have never met, and to ensure that they establish a positive relationship, is by far the biggest challenge.*

Whether the relationship is face-to-face or e-mentoring, it is normally enhanced if both parties have a measure of the other in terms of:

- general world view (ie what they feel is important in their lives)
- sense of humour (eg whether/when it is acceptable to be flippant at times)
- how strictly they will adhere to the rules on confidentiality
- what they want from the relationship
- what each can additionally offer the other
- how empathetic they will be
- what they have generally in common.

All of this *can* be established using distance media such as telephone and e-mail. However, the quality of such exchanges is subtly different from that in face-to-face meetings. (Experience from some e-learning research in the United States found that several learning pairs got along fine – until they eventually met in person. Then the relationship collapsed!) A broad ground rule for scheme co-ordinators is that they should ensure that participants who do not meet in person have a much deeper exchange of information about each other. In addition to the factual data of CVs and learning needs, it is important to tap into the emotional personality. I find the following questions to be particularly useful:

- What do you care passionately about?
- What are you most proud about in your career?
- What is your biggest fear in managing a relationship like this?
- What do enjoy most about your work?
- How would other people describe you?
- What do you enjoy most about being a mentor?
- What is your biggest ambition at work? Outside of work?
- Who do you admire, and why?

Barraging someone with such questions is not necessarily a good idea, but selecting appropriately begins the process of establishing an understanding of and respect for the other person – and this in turn reinforces rapport.

Because rapport must be maintained throughout the relationship, it is helpful for the distant mentor and mentee to get into the habit – as would be the case in a traditional face-to-face-meeting – of exchanging social information about families, children, holidays, and so on, before getting down to the nitty-gritty of the focused mentoring dialogue. Some mentoring pairs prefer to separate out these two aspects of the relationship, but most prefer to mix them.

The value of an initial face-to-face meeting before the e-mentoring relationship gets under way is illustrated by a mentoring pair of which the mentee was in Italy and the mentor in

Finland. Several months after the relationship was supposed to have started, nothing had happened, other than the exchange of a few e-mails that dealt with nothing substantive. Part of the problem lay in the fact that the mentor had just been promoted to an intensive new job in the United States and had many problems of his own to deal with. In the end, he flew to Italy, with the prime objective of meeting up with his mentee. From this initial meeting emerged very clear objectives and routines about how they were going to work together. This relationship, which was henceforth conducted mainly through e-mails and telephone, proved to be one of the strongest and most beneficial in the programme.

In many cases (perhaps most), however, there will be no opportunity to meet beforehand. This puts a great deal of initial pressure on the programme co-ordinator to make a success of the matching and to follow up each relationship closely for at least the first few weeks, to ensure that it is functioning effectively. Specific questions to both mentee and mentor about the potential, quality and tone of the relationship are important, and about the relevance of the mentor's knowledge, experience and approach. The co-ordinator may well need to intervene to ensure that one or both parties has appropriate expectations of the relationship.

In the *direction-setting* phase, clear goals for the relationship are at least as important as in a face-to-face relationship. In practice, many people find that clarity is aided by having the goals – for both parties – written down. It sometimes becomes possible to analyse what each aspect or word of a goal means in a much more systematic way than in a normal face-to-face discussion.

During the *progress-making* stage, mentors and mentees have found that it helps to establish a routine of, say, monthly semi-formal exchanges in which the mentee describes his or her progress, outlines current and/or ongoing issues, and is as specific as possible about the kind of help he or she would like. The mentor agrees to respond within a set time-frame, and both make sure they exchange dates of holidays or business trips of more than a few days so that the expectation of contact is not broken. Attention to *netiquette* (considerate conventions for e-communication) is an important element of training for both parties. Some companies have produced guidelines on netiquette as a checklist for participants.

Other issues to consider in managing this phase of the e-mentoring relationship include:

- An agreeable style of communication must be established – both mentors and mentees may need to learn how to 'muse' in text without rambling.

- As in a face-to-face meeting, it helps to establish at each interaction what the issues for discussion are, what outcomes are looked for and what kind of response the mentee is looking to the mentor to make.

- Mentees have to develop the skills of explaining issues very clearly in writing – sometimes it can be difficult to balance giving enough information for the mentor to ask appropriate questions and give relevant advice, without drowning them in detail.

- The mentor should ask the mentee to summarise (just as in face-to-face mentoring) from time to time, to ensure that they are both on the same wavelength – this is often forgotten, when communicating in text.

- Mentors sometimes find that the natural instinct to give advice, rather than help the mentee come to his or her own conclusions, is stronger when they see an issue in text. Fortunately, the extra thinking-time allowed by the medium provides space to overcome this instinct.

When it comes to *winding up*, in particular, the importance of an open review of what has been learned and achieved by both mentor and mentee, and what they have appreciated about each other's contribution to the relationship, is important in sustaining the sense of positive value and mutual respect.

At all stages in the relationship, experience by companies such as British Telecom (see case study below) suggests that using a wide range of media can enrich the relationship considerably. In addition to e-mail and telephone, there is considerable potential for fax and document exchange, for example. It can be very satisfying for a mentor to receive a text message on his or her mobile phone, 'Thanks for your help. I tried the solution we discussed, and it worked!'

CASE STUDY

E-mentoring at British Telecom

Zulfiqar Hussain

In 2001 Zulfi Hussain designed, developed and launched an e-mentoring programme under the auspices of BT's Ethnic Minority Network (EMN). The e-mentoring programme is designed to enhance the capabilities of a conventional mentoring programme, which has now been in existence for over seven years and is recognised as the largest of its kind in Europe.

BT EMN e-mentoring began as a pilot in June 2001, with four matched pairs of mentors and mentees – Belfast/Leicester, Leeds/Cardiff, Leeds/Glasgow, and Luton/Bristol – to enable good coverage of the UK.

The e-mentoring scheme was formally launched at the BT EMN annual conference of October 2001. Since then the programme has grown steadily and is currently seen as one of the most pioneering programmes of its kind, which makes full use of all the different types of technologies available such as e-mail, audio and video conferences, net meeting and even text messaging.

The aims of both the conventional and the e-mentoring programmes, explains Zulfi Hussain, is to

develop individuals and help them discover their capabilities, understand the culture of the organisation, remove barriers, break the glass ceiling, enhance their careers and achieve their full potential. However, the e-mentoring programme provides 'global reach with a local touch' by overcoming time and distance barriers, and adding a truly cross-cultural dimension.

Programme management

A small team of volunteers manages the e-mentoring programme. Each owns and manages one of the key activities, such as managing the database of participants, promoting the programme, the recruitment of mentors and mentees, and the all-important matching process.

Because the team members are spread across the UK, their meetings are generally held by regular audio conferences, but they do meet occasionally face-to-face, if and when required – for example, to resolve any issues and make improvements to the programmes.

The recruitment of mentors and mentees is done in various ways, including face-to-face discussions, adverts in internal publications, via BT's intranet and through campaigns organised by EMN and the various BT business units.

Mentors and mentees who wish to join the programme are asked to complete an online application form on the EMN website. They are asked to provide their contact details, business unit, grade, training and qualifications, achievements in the last two years, hobbies and interests, and the characteristics of the mentor/mentee with whom they wish to be matched.

Matching and support

Mentors and mentees are matched on a regular basis to achieve best results, taking into account grade, location (where appropriate), shared interests, career aspirations and development needs.

Zulfi stresses that

matches are never made merely to get people off the waiting list. The policy is to wait until a good match can be found to avoid premature failure of the mentoring relationship and any disappointment.

A letter of introduction is sent by e-mail to the mentor and mentee, asking them to make contact with each other. They are also encouraged to prepare for the first meeting to establish the ground rules of the relationship, and to agree joint aims and objectives.

The programme management team provides ongoing support for mentors and mentees via the telephone, e-mail and, if required, face-to-face meetings. Formal training workshops are also run on a regular basis.

Conventional v e-mentoring

The fundamental strategy and procedures for conventional and e-mentoring are pretty much the same, according to Zulfi, but the BT experience has shown that e-mentoring offers opportunities for mentors and mentees that would not otherwise be possible. These include:

- a global reach, which provides a greater range of cross-cultural and multinational exchange, enriching the experience of mentors, mentees and BT

- flexibility and no restrictions on time and location as a limiting factor in the matching process

- the participation of a much wider talent pool from around the world.

Monitoring and lessons learned

The e-mentoring programme is monitored using anecdotal feedback, verbal and written reports. Lessons learned to date include:

- The expectations of both the mentor and mentee must be managed carefully, to avoid disappointment.

- The roles and responsibilities of the people managing the programme must be clearly defined.

- All procedures must be robust and slot in end-to-end, and the matching process must be as efficient and as swift as possible.

- The continual 'cleansing' of the database is an absolute must.

- The programme must be promoted at every opportunity, particularly to recruit new participants.

- Ongoing monitoring and regular review is essential to evaluate the effectiveness of the programme, make improvements, and measure the benefits.

Benefits

The programme has provided considerable benefits for the mentees, mentors and BT:

- The benefits to the mentees have included improved self-confidence, learning to cope with the formal and informal structure of the company, the receipt of career advice, extensive networking opportunities, and of course managerial tutelage.

- The mentors have also gained from the mentoring relationship. Benefits have included improved job satisfaction, a greater insight into their own level of knowledge, and a new perspective on BT and on the business case for diversity (as provided by the mentee).

- There is no doubt that BT has gained by having a workforce with improved motivation, improved communications and a leadership development programme that not only develops participants but also ensures that key cultural values are passed on.

CASE STUDY

E-mentoring for small businesses

The Small Business Service (SBS) and the South-East England Development Agency (SEEDA) provided funding for Business Link Surrey to pilot an e-mentoring scheme for small businesses in 2002–2003. Designed and developed by Kevin Hunt, the South-East Regional Director for SBS, following research and evidence from the small business community, the project was evaluated by the Mentoring and Coaching Research Group at Sheffield Hallam University.

The aim of this project was to equip small business owners with a short-term (three months) burst of mentoring support on which they could subsequently build should they so wish. The mentors were experienced businesspeople drawn from the business community and the Business Volunteers Mentors Association. The programme offered mentors and mentees training in the form of a CD-ROM that introduced them to the aims of the scheme, the roles and responsibilities, and how to get the best from the relationship. More than 40 pairs took part in the pilot, and more than half of all participants responded to the evaluation survey.

Among the key results of the survey were that:

- 96 per cent of mentees and 80 per cent of mentors described the experience as positive.

- 91 per cent of mentees and 84 per cent of mentors said they would like to participate in a future programme.

- 60 per cent of mentees and 70 per cent of mentors cited convenience, flexibility and ease as the major benefits of e-mail mentoring.

- 30 per cent said they felt there was an element of impersonality about this type of mentoring.

- 50 per cent were considering continuing the relationship after the pilot period.

Quotes from participants included:

What the mentoring programme has done is 'enforced' delivery of a business plan, enabled prioritisation of different business opportunities, given me a clearer focus on what resources I need, and given me more confidence in my own business abilities.

I had been sceptical about whether I would be comfortable discussing business issues/concerns with a 'stranger' by e-mail – thinking it would be too impersonal – but I was surprised by how quickly it was possible to build a relationship of trust in this way. I believe, however, that some form of meeting would have instantly strengthened the relationship.

Among key lessons from the pilot programme was the importance of:

- appropriate matching

- goal clarity on the part of the mentee

- training for both mentors and mentees

- setting a communication plan from the beginning

- supplementing e-mail with other forms of communication

- encouragement from the mentor, to sustain the mentee's motivation.

SUMMARY & A LOOK TO THE FUTURE

The future of mentoring will involve a much broader and more intelligent use of the technologies available. There will, in particular, be much more use of video-conferencing through desktop PCs and miniature cameras. It seems likely that the majority of mentoring relationships will be hybrids of face-to-face in person, synchronous face-to-face remote, and asynchronous textual exchanges. The evidence, such as it is, suggests that this has great potential to enrich the dialogue between mentor and mentee. However, mentoring scheme co-ordinators will have to include the effective use of these technologies as an integral part of mentor and mentee training.

Part 5:

Conclusion

17

Final issues

In this relatively brief account of mentoring and how to implement a mentoring programme, we have inevitably raised a number of issues that warrant further discussion. Below we take up some of these in more detail.

ALL GOOD MENTORING RELATIONSHIPS COME TO AN END

Although one person may have several mentors, each mentoring relationship must reach the stage where it is neither needed nor wanted any longer. For this reason it is essential that every such relationship is seen from the start as a temporary alignment. Elements of it may persist, in the form of mutual aid and friendship, for many years after, but there must be clear starting- and finishing-points.

Probably the best signpost of the finishing-point is when the mentee has achieved the medium-term objectives established early on in the relationship. A spokesperson for Jewel Companies comments:

> *We feel that after a couple of years the role loses its importance and may become a more negative element than a positive one. That is, after a few years in the business it is more important that an individual be achieving on his own rather than with special help from a senior-management-level mentor.*

However it is done, the two parties must be able to back out of the arrangement without recrimination when one or both feel it is no longer beneficial.

GOOD MENTEES OFTEN MAKE GOOD MENTORS

Many of the most successful mentors are people who have experienced mentoring from the other side. Indeed, it is possible for a manager to be simultaneously mentored from above while he or she mentors someone yet more junior. One of the major difficulties in getting a mentoring programme off the ground is finding an adequate supply of mentors. Once the scheme has been going for many years, however, it automatically generates potential mentors from the ranks of former mentees. This is actually one of the litmus tests for the success of a programme – what proportion of mentees want to go on to become mentors?

OLD-STAGERS CAN BENEFIT FROM MENTORS TOO

Mentoring should not be regarded as solely for young, relatively new recruits. There are frequently people in the organisation whose development has been held back by circumstances other than ability. They may, for example, have had domestic ties that prevented them from demonstrating career ambition, particularly if they are married women. Or they may be in a cultural backwater in the company, out of the mainstream and in a staff position that has little interaction with key corporate functions. Equally, mentoring relationships can be effective between peers, or between a junior person and someone more senior.

FINDING A MENTOR WHEN THERE IS NO FORMAL MENTORING PROGRAMME

Many people progress in their companies by seeking their own mentors. By and large, senior managers are apt to be flattered if they are convinced the approach comes from someone who is capable of going a long way. The following ground rules may be useful within the corporate context:

Target one or two people as potential mentors

Talk to other people to discover their reputation within the firm. Is this person going places? Is he or she interested in developing other people? Is he or she known for teamwork? Will he or she have time for a mentoring relationship, or has he or she just been given a major project that will keep him or her out of the country for six months a year? Build up as accurate a picture as possible of each mentor candidate to establish who could be of most help to you in your career and/or personal development.

Make yourself visible

It is not who you know that counts, but who knows you. You have to make potential mentors aware of your existence. Use friends, colleagues and acquaintances to identify useful networks to join. Make a point of attending social functions, 'learning breakfasts' and other developmental events.

Show you have ambition and want to improve your abilities

Establishing the seriousness of your ambition to advance is essential. If the opportunity presents itself, get the senior manager involved in recommending training or reading that will help you expand your experience and knowledge.

Ask the potential manager formally, in person, to be your mentor

Most managers will be flattered and respond positively to an approach in person, either agreeing or making helpful suggestions on who else in the company might be more suitable.

In the latter case they will often make introductions or recommendations on your behalf. Even if you simply receive a blunt refusal, you have at least established your credentials as an ambitious employee, willing to learn.

Initial checklist

More generally, especially if you seek a mentor from the wider community, the following checklist may provide some useful starting-points:

1 What do you need a mentor for?

Try to clarify what kind of transition you want to make. Is it to a different job? A different level of competence? A different situation in life?

2 What kind of help do you want?

Do you want someone to be a sounding-board for you, to give encouragement, to provide you with a constructive challenge and expand your horizons, or to 'look out' for you, identifying opportunities and putting you forward for them? You are less likely to find someone if you are looking for a sponsor or someone to do things for you. People are much more likely to respond to a request for sharing their experience.

3 What sort of person would best be able to help you by giving advice and guidance?

Think about personality, age, experience. Think also about geography – how difficult would it be for the two of you to meet?

4 What could you bring to the relationship?

Is there any area of knowledge or experience you might usefully offer to share with a mentor?

5 Who do you know already?

Is there someone in your workplace, your local community, the church, local clubs, who you admire and feel you could learn from?

6 What networks do you belong to?

Are you a member of a professional association, an alumni club, a chamber of commerce, a sports association or similar organisation? They may already have a mentoring scheme, or be willing to put you in touch with potential mentors on an ad hoc basis.

7 Are there mentor registers you can sign on to?

A variety of organisations – including some TECs, charities and community organisations – provide a matching service for specific categories of people.

8 Can you identify someone you could approach who is very well networked and could refer you either directly to potential mentors or to organisations that can help?

Someone in any of the organisations above might be able to help you in this way. Other useful people to consider approaching include personnel professionals, senior managers, academic tutors, pastors and career consultants.

9 How will you make the approach?

It is often easier when someone else makes the introduction. If you have to take the first steps yourself, however, spend some time rehearsing what you have to say. Be confident – the worst that can happen is that the person says no. In practice, most people are sufficiently flattered and respond very positively to requests that they should become a mentor.

10 How will you translate good intentions into deeds?

Aim to put the date for the first formal mentoring meeting into the diary as soon as he or she agrees to consider the relationship. Do not be the one to postpone the meeting – that may undo all your good work. Above all, be considerate of the mentor's time and goodwill – make it clear how pleased you are that he or she has accepted.

Appendix 1

The evolution of modern mentoring

Although mentoring is a concept that has only recently entered into the general vocabulary of business and society, it has a long pedigree. The word 'mentor' originally comes from Greek mythology. Odysseus, before setting out for the Trojan War, entrusted his son to the care and direction of his old and trusted friend Mentor. (In fact, Mentor was not particularly helpful. It was the goddess Athena who was young Telemachus's real mentor.) Yet in spite of the variety of definitions of mentoring (and the variety of names given to it, from coaching or counselling to sponsorship) all the experts and communicators appear to agree that modern mentoring has its origins in the concept of apprenticeship. In the days when the guilds ruled the commercial world, the road to the top in business began with an early apprenticeship to the master craftsman, a trader, or a ship's captain. This older, more experienced individual passed down his knowledge of how the task was done and how to operate in the commercial world.

Intimate personal relationships frequently developed between the master (or mentor) and the apprentice (or learner), especially as the apprentice acquired skills and began to substitute for his mentor. Marrying the master's daughter became an accepted means of providing career progression and retaining key skills with the firm.

The Industrial Revolution altered this emphasis, demanding large numbers of recruits, which swamped personalised attention. Apprenticeship often degenerated to the stage where it involved depersonalised mass training in technical areas. Within the large corporation there grew up informal, often hidden, methods of passing on the experience of old-timers to young recruits. At the lower levels, a supervisor might 'keep an eye on' a promising employee. Senior managers might identify a potential high-flyer and provide him or her with confidential advice and encouragement. Although the term might not itself have had currency, therefore, mentoring was nonetheless at work.

In recent years, mentoring has also spread beyond the world of careers and work to embrace a wide spectrum of community needs. In the UK, for example, there are active mentoring programmes to help disadvantaged schoolchildren and university students to stick at and concentrate on their studies, young offenders to change their lives, teenage mothers to cope with their multiple responsibilities, and head teachers to improve the management of their schools. Now there are programmes to help the unemployed of all ages into the workforce.

There are also schemes to encourage creativity in the arts and sciences, and to support owner-entrepreneurs in developing their own competence in line with the increasing demands of their businesses.

The idea of formalising all this came from the United States, in the late 1970s, when a number of companies saw the potential in making this kind of sponsorship and guidance available to all their potential high-flying young men. It did not take long for other people to realise the possibilities of transferring this process into the wider community, and there soon came an explosion of community schemes, aimed in particular at young people at risk and young people from disadvantaged backgrounds, with the aim of helping them build meaningful and useful lives. Inevitably, some of these had a diversity dimension to them, and mentoring gradually became co-opted to support programmes of positive action, both racial and gender-based.

Europe and Australasia were not far behind. But initial experiments with mentoring were often disappointing. Although sponsoring mentoring was acceptable informally, European business cultures resisted the idea of such overt godfathering behaviour. A very different style of mentoring evolved in employment – one in which the mentor's power and authority were not central to the relationship (although the mentor's experience was). In European, developmental mentoring, the relationship became a source of mutual support and learning. The role of the mentor was and is to enable the mentee to become independent as quickly as possible. (So big was this difference that European organisations dropped the US term *protégé* because it implied too many of the wrong associations.) Community and academic mentoring remains a mixture of sponsoring and developmental mentoring, depending on practical experience and where the scheme organisers have taken their working model from. Many of the most extensive schemes – such as that to provide mentors from business for headteachers – now operate as peer learning exchanges.

The sheer range of mentoring schemes now in operation is enormous. Children as young as five are being mentored by older children between nine and 11. Thousands of children who have difficulty learning to read or write are being helped by learning mentors (although, as the scheme is currently structured, these are not really mentors but coaches/instructors). Gifted children are being helped to stick with their talents – for example, as musicians – by pairing up with retired professionals whose enthusiasm helps carry them through the many other distractions that assail teenagers. Black students at risk of giving up on their university studies are being supported by businesspeople. Other students are mentoring disabled or socially excluded pupils to help them make the transition into work or further education.

Once they do make it into the world of work, many people also find there is a mentor available to support them. We have helped dozens of companies establish programmes for their graduate and other young recruits. The benefits have been remarkable, especially in terms of the retention of this valuable talent. Mentoring has now become a standard part of the support for people taking professional qualifications – for example, in nursing or engineering. New teachers and experienced teachers who are having problems in the classroom can expect to have a mentor in many schools.

As people rise through the ranks of an organisation, at every major transition stage – such as their first supervisory role – a mentor can and often does provide an anchor for the tough decisions they have to make. One of the hardest transitions of all is for mothers returning to work after maternity leave. The emotional trauma involved in leaving the baby and re-establishing working relationships and skills can be greatly eased through mentoring from another mum who has been through the same experience.

There is now a wide range of mentoring schemes aimed at small businesses, from the very general to specific areas such as exporting. These help the entrepreneur put emphasis on his or her own growth as well as that of the business. Executives in business, public service and education are one of the fastest-growing audiences for mentoring – the lonelier and more complex the job at the top becomes, the greater the need for a sympathetic, knowledgeable but non-partisan sounding-board becomes. Other schemes we have been involved in in recent years include GPs starting to practise in drug addiction, successful asylum-seekers and artists. There have even been schemes to mentor people through the difficult transition into retirement.

In short, wherever you look, there is an increasing variety of applications of mentoring.

With all this diversity, one of the problems is a lack of effective integration, sharing of good practice and sharing of resources. Community, business and academic mentoring all follow their own routes.

My vision of ultimate mentoring is that everyone will have an opportunity to participate in and benefit from mentoring throughout their lives – that it will become a natural substitute for the extended family of village communities in previous centuries. I was gratified to hear recently of a school which had eliminated bullying by making every senior form responsible for mentoring pupils in junior forms. The cascade effect is very powerful.

We know that people who have positive experience of being a mentee typically make good and committed mentors. All we have to do is tap that enthusiasm. Instead of mentoring happening at rare, widely separated periods in our lives, in a mentoring community everyone would be mentor or mentee simultaneously for much of their lives. Because the vast majority of people who experience being a mentor find the role intensely fulfilling, this is not a pipedream.

Of course, there is a lot of work to do before such a vision is even partly realised. The vast amount of good practice out there is not integrated – and there is a lot of very bad practice, especially in executive mentoring. There are UK standards for mentoring in schools and youth justice, and international standards for mentoring in employment. They are not linked as yet.

There is considerable confusion over what the word 'mentor' means. It is variously confused with 'coach', 'counsellor', 'teaching assistant', 'big brother' and 'godfather'. In some circumstances the mentor has an authority role (eg some youth justice schemes, in which the mentor might be responsible for returning a young person to custody); in most developmental mentoring relationships, this would be unconscionable. The nature of the role and the clarity of understanding of the role by both parties in a mentoring relationship has a major impact on its success or failure.

Nor does it help that the quality of much academic research in the area is poor. Failure to define what is being measured is just one of these quality problems. This has led to great difficulties in determining how formal or informal a mentoring relationship should be. There has to be some structure, to provide a sense of purpose and, in the case of young or vulnerable people, a protective framework. But relationships also have to operate with a high degree of flexibility and personal rapport. Getting the balance right is a major challenge for scheme organisers.

Another challenge is balancing the need to stretch mentees against the need to provide support for them. Equipping mentors with the instinctive competence to adapt the challenge level to individual needs and circumstances is not easy – but it is essential in establishing relationships that will deliver results.

Appendix 2

Making the business case

The six 'slides' below (originally PowerPoint slides to be utilised as visual aids for a screen presentation using an overhead projector) provide a helpful aide-mémoire when making the business case in the form of a verbal presentation to the top team.

Slide 1

Mentoring delivers …

- reduced costs and increased effectiveness of recruitment

- massive improvements in retention (people with mentors are up to 13 times less likely to leave)

- higher productivity (eg 20% for salespeople)

- improvements in communication, motivation and succession planning

---

Slide 2

Who gains from mentoring?

- the mentee – rapid learning and constructive challenge; availability of advice and sounding-board

- the mentor – an opportunity to practise development skills, to be challenged, and to reflect upon own practice

- the line manager – the mentee learns how to manage him/her better

---

Slide 3

> Mentoring and employee retention
>
> Allied Irish Banks
>
> - hires 200 graduates a year
> - before the mentoring programme, was losing 25% of graduates in their first 12 months
> - with the mentoring programme, is losing only 8% in the first 12 months

Slide 4

> Big brothers/big sisters
>
> 10–16-year-olds from deprived backgrounds, who had a mentor:
>
> - were 46% less likely to begin drug use (70% for minorities)
> - were 27% less likely to begin drinking
> - were 30% less likely to hit someone
> - skipped 80% fewer schooldays
> - had improved academic performance and attitude
> - had improved relationships with parents and peers
>
> US study by PPV (Nov 1995)

Slide 5

> The benefits of mentoring:
>
> The Norwegian women's leaders programme
>
> - 84% of mentees are more secure in their leadership role
> - 55% of mentors are more secure in their leadership role
> - 91% of mentors say they have learned much from the relationship with their mentee
> - 90% of both mentors and mentees are more conscious of their own values
> - 80% of both report that they have developed personally
> - 82% of mentees report that the programme has had a positive effect on career development

Slide 6

The bottom line

Mentoring

- develops two for the cost of one
- provides learning 'just in time'
- is essential to a firm's being an 'employer of choice'
- produces long-term sustainable benefit
- is essential to developing a learning culture
- provides a payback that is both immediate and long-term

Bibliography

ALLEMAN E. (1984) *What's Really True About Mentoring?* Mentor, Ohio, Leadership Development Consultants Inc

ALLEMAN E. (1994) 'Interpersonal perceptions in mentoring relationships'. Paper to American Educational Research Annual Meeting, New Orleans

ALLEMAN E., COCHRAN J., DOVERSPIKE J. and NEWMAN I. (1984) 'Enriching mentoring relationships', *The Personnel and Guidance Journal*, Vol 62: 329–332

ALRED G. and GARVEY R. (1996) 'Approaching mentoring: becoming a semi-god'. Proceedings of the Third European Mentoring Conference, London

ANTAL A. B. (1993) 'Odysseus' legacy to management development: mentoring', *European Management Journal*, Vol 11, No 4

ARYEE S. and CHAY Y. W. (1994) 'An examination of the impact of career-oriented mentoring on work commitment, attitudes and career satisfaction among professionals and managerial employees', *British Journal of Management*, Vol 5: 241–9

ARYEE S., WYATT T. and STONE R. (1996) 'Early career outcomes of graduate employees: the effect of mentoring and ingratiation', *Journal of Management Studies*, Vol 33, No 1

BARHAM K. and CONWAY C. (1997) 'Mentoring goes international', *Ashridge Journal*, March

BARHAM K. and CONWAY C. (1998) *Developing Business and People Internationally – A mentoring approach.* Berkhampsted, Ashridge Research

BAXTER A. G. and CLARK K. M. (1992) 'Positive and productive mentoring: inside views', *Mentoring International*, Vol 6, Nos 2/3, spring/summer

BEATTIE R. S. and McDOUGALL M. (1995) 'Peer mentoring: the issues and outcomes of non-hierarchical developmental relationships'. Paper to British Academy of Management Annual Conference

BENNETTS C. (1995) 'The secrets of a good relationship', *People Management,* 30 June

BENNETTS C. (1998) *A Pilot Inquiry into Current Mentoring Projects and Programmes for Unemployed Youth in England, Scotland and Wales.* Hertfordshire TEC

BENNETTS C. (1999a) 'Interpersonal aspects of informal mentor/learner relationships: a research perspective'. Proceedings of the European Mentoring Centre Conference, London, November

BENNETTS C. (1999b) 'Mentoring relationships and young people: trend and tradition in mentoring'. National Youth Agency/DfEE/Rowntree, Research, Policy and Practice Forum on Young People, London

BERGLAS S. (2002) 'The very real dangers of executive coaching', *Harvard Business Review*, 1 June

BLAKE R. R. and MOUTON J. S. (1964) *The Managerial Grid*. Houston, TX, Gulf

BROWN S. (2000) 'The keys to successful mentoring in SmithKline Beecham'. Proceedings of the Seventh annual European Mentoring Conference, Cambridge, November

BUREAU OF BUSINESS PRACTICE (1990) 'Being a mentor', *Management Letter* 304, February

BURKE R. J. and McKEEN C. A. (1997) 'Benefits of mentoring relationships among managerial and professional women: a cautionary tale', *Journal of Vocational Behaviour*, Vol 51

BURKE R. J., McKENNA C. S. and McKEEN C. A. (1991) 'How do mentorships differ from typical supervisory relationships?', *Psychological Review*, Vol 68

CARTER S. (1993) 'Developing an organisation mentoring scheme', *Professional Manager*, pp15–16

CARTER S. and LEWIS G. (1994) 'The four bases of mentoring'. Proceedings of the First European Mentoring Conference, European Mentoring Centre/Sheffield Business School

CARUSO R. (ed.) (1992) *Mentoring and the Business Environment: Asset or liability?* Brookfield, VT, Dartmouth Publishing

CHAO G. T. (1997) 'Mentoring phases and outcomes', *Journal of Vocational Behavior*, Vol 51: 15–28

CHAO G. T. (1998) 'Invited reaction: challenging research in mentoring', *Human Resource Development Quarterly*, Vol 9, No 4, winter

CHAO G. T., WALZ P. M. and GARDNER P. D. (1992) 'Formal and informal mentorships: a comparison on mentoring functions and contrast with non-mentored counterparts', *Personnel Psychology*, Vol 45: 619–36

CLUTTERBUCK D. (1992) *Top Manager Programme*. Oxford Regional Health Authority

CLUTTERBUCK D. (1993) *Mentoring – A Key Tool in Training and Development: Current best practice*. London, The Industrial Society

CLUTTERBUCK D. (1994a) 'Blooming managers', *Management Training*, February

CLUTTERBUCK D. (1994b) 'Business mentoring in evolution', *Mentoring,* summer

CLUTTERBUCK D. (1994c) 'Managing mentoring, how to avoid the common pitfalls', *Mentoring and Coaching*. Deventer, Netherlands, Kluwer Bedrijfswetenschappen

CLUTTERBUCK D. (1994d) 'The mentoring game', *The Business Magazine,* October

CLUTTERBUCK D. (1994e) 'Uncovering the way a mentor does his work', *The Business Magazine*, November

CLUTTERBUCK D. (1995) *Consenting Adults*. London, Channel Four Publications

CLUTTERBUCK D. (1996a) 'Developing learning teams', *Training Officer*, Vol 32, No. 6, July/August

CLUTTERBUCK D. (1996b) 'How executives learn from each other', in P. Sadler (ed.) *International Executive Development Programmes*. London, Kogan Page

CLUTTERBUCK D. (1996c) 'Will you be my mentor?', *Modern Management*, Vol 10, June

CLUTTERBUCK D. (1997a) 'Are you getting in the way of the learning organisation?', *Direction*, April

CLUTTERBUCK D. (1997b) 'Mentoring and the glass ceiling', *The Diversity Directory*, 12th edition. Bedford, Diversity UK

CLUTTERBUCK D. (1997c) *Power in the Mentoring Relationship*. Birmingham, Staff and Educational Development Association

CLUTTERBUCK D. (1998a) *Learning Alliances*. London, Institute of Personnel and Development

CLUTTERBUCK D. (1998b) 'The rapid rise of executive mentoring', *Croner's Human Resources Briefing*, 12 January

CLUTTERBUCK D. (1999a) 'Mentoring, developing two for the price of one', in J. Prior MBE (ed.) *Gower Handbook of Training and Development*, 3rd edition. Aldershot, Gower

CLUTTERBUCK D. (1999b) 'Mentoring in business, executives and directors', *Mentoring and Tutoring*, Vol 6, No 3

CLUTTERBUCK D. (2000a) 'Ten core mentor competencies', *Organisations and People*, Vol 7, No 2, November

CLUTTERBUCK D. (2000b) 'Where next in mentoring?', *AMED News*, October

CLUTTERBUCK D. (2000/2001) 'Quiet transformation, the growing power of mentoring', *Mount Eliza Business Review*, summer/autumn

CLUTTERBUCK D. and DEVINE M. (1987) *Businesswoman*. London, Macmillan

CLUTTERBUCK D. and MEGGINSON D. (1999a) *Mentoring Executives and Directors*. Oxford, Butterworth-Heinemann

CLUTTERBUCK D. and MEGGINSON D. (1999b) *Mentoring in Action*. London, Kogan Page

CLUTTERBUCK D. and MEGGINSON M. (2001) 'Winding up or winding down?' Proceedings of the European Mentoring Centre Conference, Cambridge (UK), November

CLUTTERBUCK D. and MEGGINSON M. (2003) 'Winding up or winding down a mentoring relationship'. Research article available at www.clutterbuckassociates.com

CLUTTERBUCK D. and RAGINS B. R. (2001) *Mentoring and Diversity: An international perspective*. Oxford, Butterworth-Heinemann

CLUTTERBUCK D. and RAGINS B. R. (2001) *Mentoring and Diversity: An international perspective*. Oxford, Butterworth-Heinemann

CLUTTERBUCK D. and SCHNEIDER S. (1998) 'Executive mentoring', *Croner's Executive Companion Bulletin*, issue 29, October

CLUTTERBUCK D. and SNOW D. (1995) *BEAT – Beginning Education and Training: An evaluation*. Birmingham, BEAT Projects

CLUTTERBUCK D. and SWEENEY J. (2003) 'Apart or together: good practice in training mentors and mentees', *Clutterbuck Associates newsletter*, September

CLUTTERBUCK D. and WYNNE B. (1993) 'Mentoring and coaching', in A. Mumford (ed.) *Handbook of Management Development*. Aldershot, Gower

CMSI (2001) Mentoring Programme Benchmark 2000 Survey. Corporate Mentoring Solutions Inc. Available from EMCC library

COLLIN A. (1979) 'Notes on some typologies of management development and the role of the mentor in the process of adaptation of the individual to the organisation', *Personnel Review*, Vol 8, No 1

CONWAY C. (1995) 'Mentoring in the mainstream', *Directions – the Ashridge Journal*, April

CONWAY C. (1998) *Strategies for Mentoring*. Chichester, John Wiley

CROSBY F. J. (1999) 'The development literature on developmental relationships', in A. J. Murrell, F. J. Crosby and R. J. Ely (eds) *Mentoring Dilemmas: Developmental relationships within multicultural organizations*. Mahwah, NJ. Lawrence Erlbaum Associates

CUNNINGHAM J. B. and EBERLE T. (1993) 'Characteristics of the mentoring experience: a qualitative study', *Personnel Review*, Vol 22, No 4

DARLING L. A. (1984) 'Mentor types and life cycles', *The Journal of Nursing Administration*, November

EBY L. T. (1997) 'Alternative forms of mentoring in changing organizational environments: a conceptual extension of the mentoring literature', *Journal of Vocational Behavior*, Vol 51: 125–44

ENGSTRÖM T. (1997/1978) 'Personality factors' impact on success in the mentor-protégé relationship'. MSc thesis for Norwegian School of Hotel Management, Oslo

EQUAL OPPORTUNITIES REVIEW (1985) *Equal Opportunities Review*, No 60, March/April

FAGAN M. (1988) 'The term "mentor": a review of the literature', *International Journal of Mentoring*, Vol 2, No 12, winter

FAGENSON-ELAND E. A., MARKS M. A. and AMENDOLA K. I. (1997) 'Perceptions of mentoring relationships', *Journal of Vocational Behaviour*, Vol 51: 29–42

FORRET M. L., TURBAN D. B. and DOUGHERTY T. W. (1996) 'Issues facing organisations when implementing formal mentoring programmes', *Leadership and Organization Journal*, Vol 17, No 3

GARDNER C. E. (1996) 'Mentoring: a study of the concept, theory and practice of mentoring in the educational field'. Dissertation for MA in Education at the University of Central England, Birmingham

GARDNER C. (1997) 'Mentoring: a professional friendship?' Proceedings of the Fourth European Conference on Mentoring, European Mentoring Centre/Sheffield Business School

GARVEY R. (1995) 'Healthy signs for mentoring', *Education and Training*, Vol 37, No 5

GARVEY R. (1998) 'Mentoring in the marketplace: studies of learning at work'. Thesis submitted for the degree of Doctor of Philosophy, Durham University

GARVEY R. (1999) 'Mentoring and the changing paradigm', *Mentoring and Tutoring*, Vol 7, No 1

GARVEY R. and ALRED G. (2000a) 'Developing mentors', *Career Development International*, Vol 5, Nos 4/5: 216–22

GARVEY R. and ALRED G. (2000b) 'Educating mentors', *Mentoring and Tutoring*, Vol 8, No 2

GARVEY R. and ALRED G. (2001) 'Mentoring and the tolerance of complexity', *Futures*, Vol 33, No 5

GARVEY R., ALRED G. and SMITH R. (1996) 'First person mentoring', *Career Development International*, Vol 1, No 5

GIBB S. (1994a) 'Evaluating mentoring', *Education and Training*, Vol 36, No 5

GIBB S. (1994b) 'Inside corporate mentoring schemes, the development of a conceptual framework', *Personnel Review*, Vol 23, No 3

GIBB S. (1999) 'The usefulness of theory: a case study in evaluating formal mentoring schemes', *Human Relations*, Vol 52, No 2, August

GIBB S. and MEGGINSON D. (1992) 'Inside corporate mentoring schemes, a new agenda of concerns', *Personnel Review*, Vol 21, No 7

GRAY W. A. (1986) 'Achieving employment equity and affirmative action through formalized mentoring'. Proceedings of the National Conference on Management in the Public Sector, Victoria, BC, Canada, 21–23 April

HAMILTON R. (1993) *Mentoring*. London, The Industrial Society

HAY J. (1993) 'A new approach to mentoring', *Financial Training Review*, October

HAY J. (1995) *Transformational Mentoring: Creating developmental alliances for changing organizational cultures*. Maidenhead, McGraw-Hill

HAY J. (1997) *Action Mentoring: Creating your own developmental alliance*. Watford, Sherwood

HAY J. (1998) 'Mentoring – traditional versus developmental', *Organisations and People*, Vol 5, No 3, August

HODGSON P. (1987) 'Managers can be taught but leaders have to learn', *Industrial and Commercial Training*, November-December

HOLLOWAY A. (1994) *Mentoring: The definitive workbook*. Manchester, Development Processes

HUNT D. M. (1992) 'A longitudinal study of mentor outcomes', *Mentoring International*, Vol 6, Nos 2/3, spring

IBARRA H. (2000) 'Making partner: a mentor's guide to the psychological journey', *Harvard Business Review*, Vol 78, No 2

INDUSTRIAL SOCIETY (1995) 'Managing development throughout the hierarchy', *Training Management*, Vol 8, No 4

INDUSTRIAL SOCIETY AND THE ITEM GROUP (1990) *The Line Manager's Role in Developing Talent*. London, Industrial Society

KIZILOS P. (1990) 'Take my mentor, please', *Training*, April

KLASEN N. and CLUTTERBUCK D. (2001) *Implementing Mentoring Schemes*. Oxford, Butterworth-Heinemann

KRAM K. (1980) 'Mentoring processes at work: developmental relationships in managerial careers'. Doctoral dissertation, Yale University

KRAM K. (1983) 'Phases of the mentor relationship', *Academy of Management Journal*, Vol 26, No 4

KRAM K. (1985a) 'Improving the mentoring process', *Training and Development Journal*, April

KRAM K. (1985b) *Mentoring at Work*. Lanham, MD, University Press of America

KRAM K. and ISABELLA L. A. (1985) 'Mentoring alternatives: the role of peer relationships in career development', *Academy of Management Journal*, March

LEVINSON D. (1978) *The Seasons of a Man's Life*. New York, Alfred Knopf

LEWIS G. (1988) *The Mentoring Manager: Strategies for fostering talent and spreading knowledge*. London, Pitman/Institute of Management

LEWIS G. (1993) *The Mentoring Manager*. London, Pitman

LIKERT R. (1961) *New Patterns of Management*. New York, McGraw-Hill

MacLENNAN N. (1995) *Coaching and Mentoring*. Aldershot, Gower

McDOUGALL M and BEATTIE R. S. (1997) 'Peer mentoring at work', *Management Learning*, Vol 28, No 4

McGREGOR L. (2000) 'Mentoring: the Australian experience'. Proceedings of the Seventh European Mentoring Conference, Cambridge, November

MEGGINSON D. (1993) 'Three ways of mentoring'. AMED/Sundridge Park Conference Proceedings

MEGGINSON D. (1994a) 'Images of mentoring'. EMC Research Conference, Sheffield

MEGGINSON D. (1994b) 'Planned and emergent learning, a framework and a method', *Executive Development*, Vol 7, No 6

MEGGINSON D. (2000) 'Current issues in mentoring', *Career Development International*, Vol 5, No 45

MEGGINSON D. and CLUTTERBUCK D. (1995) *Mentoring in Action: A practical guide for managers*. London, Kogan Page

MUMFORD A. (1985) 'What's new in management development', *Personnel Management*, May

MURRAY M., with OWEN M. A. (1991) *Beyond the Myths and Magic of Mentoring*. San Francisco, Jossey-Bass

NOE R. A. (1988) 'An investigation of the determinants of successful assigned mentoring relationships', *Personnel Psychology*, Vol 41: 457–79

NOLLER R. B. (1982) 'Mentoring: a renaissance of apprenticeship', *Journal of Creative Behaviour*, Vol 16

O'NEILL R. M, HORTON S. and CROSBY F. J. (1999) 'Gender issues in developmental relationships', in A. J. Murrell, F. J. Crosby and R. J. Ely (eds) *Mentoring Dilemmas: Developmental relationships within multicultural organizations*. Mahwah, NJ, Lawrence Erlbaum Associates

ORPEN C. (1997) 'The effects of formal mentoring on employee work motivation, organizational commitment and job performance', *The Learning Organization*, Vol 4, No 2

PARSLOE E. (1992) *Coaching, Mentoring and Assessing: A practical guide to developing competence*. London, Kogan Page

PARSLOE E. (1999) 'A selection of letters', *People Management*, 20 May

RAGINS B. R. (1997a) 'Antecedents of diversified mentoring relationships', *Journal of Vocational Behaviour*, Vol 51

RAGINS B. R (1997b) 'Diversified mentoring relationships in organisations: a power perspective', *Academy of Management Review*, Vol 22, No 2

RAGINS B. R. (1999a) 'Where do we go from here? And how do we get there? Methodological issues in conducting research on diversity and mentoring relationships', in A. J. Murrell, F. J. Crosby and R. J. Ely (eds) *Mentoring Dilemmas: Developmental relationships within multicultural organizations*. Mahwah, NJ, Lawrence Erlbaum Associates

RAGINS B. R. (1999b) 'Gender and mentoring relationships' in G. N. Powell (ed.) *Handbook of Gender and Work*. Thousand Oaks, CA/London, Sage

RAGINS B. R. and COTTON J. L. (1993) 'Gender and willingness to mentor in organisations', *Academy of Management Journal*, Vol 19, September

RAGINS B. R. and COTTON J. L. (1996) 'Jumping the hurdles: the barriers to mentoring for women in organisations', *Leadership and Organisation Development Journal*, Vol 17, No 3

RAGINS B. R. and COTTON J. L. (1999) 'Mentor functions and outcomes: a comparison of men and women in formal and informal mentoring relationships', *Journal of Applied Psychology*, Vol 84, No 4

RAGINS B. R. and McFARLIN D. B. (1990) 'Perceptions of mentoring roles in cross-gender mentoring relationships', *Journal of Vocational Behaviour*, Vol 37

RAGINS B. R. and SCANDURA T. A. (1993) 'The effects of sex and gender role orientation on mentorship in male dominated occupations', *Journal of Vocational Behaviour*, Vol 43

RAGINS B. R. and SCANDURA T. A. (1994) 'Gender differences in expected outcomes of mentoring relationships', *Academy of Management Journal*, Vol 37, No 4

RAGINS B. R. and SCANDURA T. A. (1999) 'Burden or blessing? Expected costs and benefits of being a mentor', *Journal of Organisational Behaviour*, Vol 20

RAGINS B. R., COTTON J. L. and MILLER J. S. (2000) 'Marginal mentoring: the effects of type of mentor, quality of relationship and program design on work and career attitudes', *Academy of Management Journal*, Vol 43, No 6

SCHRIESHEIM C. A. and MURPHY C. J. (1976) 'Relationships between leader behaviour and subordinate satisfaction and performance: a test of some situational moderators', *Journal of Applied Psychology*, Vol 61, No 5

SEGERMAN-PECK L. (1991) *Networking and Mentoring: A woman's guide*. London, Piatkus

SIEBERT S. (1999) 'The effectiveness of facilitated mentoring: a longitudinal quasi-experiment', *Journal of Vocational Behavior*, Vol 54

SMIT A. (2000) 'Transformational mentoring: to implement an action learning process in developing effective mentoring practice'. Doctoral thesis, Southern Cross University, Australia

SMITH P. and WEST-BURNHAM J. (eds) (1993) *Mentoring in the Effective School*. Harlow, Longman

STOTT A. and SWEENEY J. (1999) 'More than a match', *People Management*, 30 June

STRUTHERS N. J. (1995) 'Differences in mentoring: a function of gender or organizational rank?', *Journal of Social Behaviour and Personality*, Vol 10

THOMAS D. A. (1990) 'The impact of race on managers' experience of developmental relationships (mentoring and sponsorship): an intra-organizational study', *Journal of Organizational Behaviour*, Vol 11

TURBAN D. B. and DOUGHERTY T. W. (1994) 'Role of protégé personality in receipt of mentoring and career success', *Academy of Management Journal*, Vol 37, No 3

VIATOR R. E. (1999) 'An analysis of formal mentoring programs and perceived barriers to obtaining a mentor at large public accounting firms', *Accounting Horizons*, Vol 13, No 1

WALES S. (1998) 'Executive mentoring: a retrospective exploration of managers' experiences of external mentoring'. Dissertation for MSc in Change Agent Skills and Strategies, University of Surrey

WILKIN M. (ed) (1992) *Mentoring in Schools*. London, Kogan Page

WRIGHT R. G and WERTHER W. B. (1991) 'Mentors at work', *Journal of Management Development*, Vol 10, No 3

ZEY M. G. (1984) *The Mentor Connection*. New York, Dow Jones Irwin

Index